Praise for
Where Will You Go from Here?

"Valorie Burton navigates us through the maze of life's uncertainty with the skill of a GPS system placing us back on course. For those who refuse to live the rest of their lives stuck on the side of the road, this book gives guidance!"

—BISHOP T. D. JAKES, *New York Times* best-selling author,
founder and senior pastor of The Potter's House

"This compelling book offers a hands-on approach to recovering—and thriving—after crisis. Valorie Burton provides well-researched solutions, practical help, and many examples of real people who have faced dark times of adversity and come out on the other end stronger for it. In these pages, readers will find hope and answers for how to progress from a place of pain and setback to hope and abundant life."

—SHAUNTI FELDHAHN, best-selling author of *For Women Only*

"If you are in that 'what now?' place in your life, this is the book for you—filled with practical steps and profound principles to jump-start your comeback, but even more important, you're repositioning for new levels of victory in your life. Valorie Burton speaks from experience as well as learned wisdom and offers the tools you need to master your life and get the results you desire."

—MICHELLE McKINN
How to Make Life W

"I've never seen such a clear ro   Burton
has so vividly drawn in this pheno   lp you
arrive at a better destination; she inspires you to savor the journey every

step of the way. I'll be using *Where Will You Go from Here?* with many of my coaching clients!"

—SHANNON ETHRIDGE, M.A., certified life coach, international
speaker, and best-selling author of *Every Woman's Battle*

"In *Where Will You Go from Here?* my friend Valorie Burton offers a clear, concise, and manageable plan for dealing with the curve balls that life throws at you. If you open your mind to receive what she has laid out, you will be much more prepared to make the right choices at the right time."

—ROLAND S. MARTIN, host/managing editor of *Washington
Watch* (TV One cable network) and analyst for CNN
and the *Tom Joyner Morning Show*

"In her book *Where Will You Go from Here?* Valorie Burton has provided us with the perfect map for those times when we feel traumatized and can't see the road in front of us. I am excited she has put her words of wisdom on paper. If an unexpected challenge has brought your life to a screeching halt, Valorie will help get you moving again!"

—CHONDA PIERCE, comedienne, author, and recording artist

Where Will You Go from Here?

Where Will You Go from Here?

Moving Forward
When Life Doesn't
Go as Planned

Valorie Burton

WATERBROOK
PRESS

WHERE WILL YOU GO FROM HERE?
PUBLISHED BY WATERBROOK PRESS
12265 Oracle Boulevard, Suite 200
Colorado Springs, Colorado 80921

Details in some anecdotes and stories have been changed to protect the identities of the persons involved.

ISBN 978-0-307-72976-7
ISBN 978-0-307-72977-4 (electronic)

Cover design by Mark Ford; cover photo by Jackie Hicks

Published in association with the literary agency of Alive Communications Inc., 7680 Goddard Street, Suite 200, Colorado Springs, Colorado 80920, www.alivecommunications.com.

Published in the United States by WaterBrook Multnomah, an imprint of the Crown Publishing Group, a division of Random House Inc., New York.

WATERBROOK and its deer colophon are registered trademarks of Random House Inc.

Library of Congress Cataloging-in-Publication Data on file with the Library of Congress.

Printed in the United States of America
2011—First Edition

10 9 8 7 6 5 4 3 2 1

Contents

Things turn out best for the people who make the best of the way things turn out.

—JOHN WOODEN

ONE

This Isn't the Way You Planned It

When Your World Turns Upside Down

Life has a way of taking us by surprise. One day everything seems fine. You're making progress toward your professional and financial goals, you're finally getting in shape, you're making plans for the future, and *bam,* you're knocked senseless by some unexpected development. Suddenly everything you believed to be true about your life is in question. You're disoriented. You're scared. And you may feel as if you've landed in a foreign, lonely place.

My guess is you picked up this book because you know exactly what I'm talking about. Some unexpected turn in your life story has left you not only deeply disappointed but also unsure of what do to next. So my goal is to help you answer this vital question: where will you go from here? Whatever has sent your life plans careening off course—an unplanned career change, the death of a marriage, a health crisis, or something else altogether—I've written this book with your unique emotions, challenges, and destiny in mind.

As a personal and executive coach, I have worked with many clients around the world, and one thing I know for sure: when you ask the right questions, you get the right answers. The answers you are looking for will require you to be honest, open, and courageous—courageous enough to rise to the challenges you face despite your fears. I believe you can do it. And I will walk with you every step of the way—from helping you assess where you are now to encouraging you to confidently step onto your new path and to pay it forward by serving others with your newfound wisdom.

In the following pages you'll encounter people who, like you, have smacked up against painful and unexpected challenges, yet they've found a way to not only recover from their setbacks but actually press through adversity to find a better path for their lives:

- Roland was on track in his career when he suddenly lost his job. From there life became a downward spiral: divorce, medical emergency, and bankruptcy fell like dominoes over the next two years. In his own words, he'll share how he made a seemingly impossible comeback. Better yet, he tells how his setbacks propelled him to higher heights than he's ever reached before.

- Jacqueline was a twenty-eight-year-old mom, recently separated, when she was blindsided by a devastating seizure that changed the course of her life, as well as her daughter's. Her dark, lonely journey to recovery lasted more than a decade—but it yields powerful inspiration for your own journey as you discover how the setback that almost ended her life ultimately saved her.

- Claire was a successful forty-something woman earning a six-figure salary when she met and married the man of her dreams—or so she thought. In the span of a year, she lost her life savings, her marriage, and her mother. How could she navigate it all—and even recover from her losses—

without becoming bitter or overwhelmed? The answer is one all of us need to hear.

- Kevin was an all-star athlete whose athletic abilities landed him a full-ride scholarship to college. But shortly after his arrival on campus, a devastating accident left him paralyzed. So how is it possible that he could confidently pursue—and achieve—the full and satisfying life he'd always dreamed of? The unforgettable story of Kevin's resilience will give you renewed hope for your future.

What does your own setback look like? Whatever it is you have experienced, I'm sure of two things:

1. Right now your life isn't the way you planned it.
2. You have the inner strength to get through this—and to grow through this.

How can I be so sure? Not only have I coached numerous others onto their own path to recovery, I have also personally learned from my own setbacks that all things truly do work together for good—when we walk on in faith.

My Story

As a personal and executive coach, people often come to me for a life makeover. But at times I've had to coach myself through my own makeover—forging into new territory, allowing my authentic self to emerge, and embracing frightening uncertainty with hope and faith. I understand what it feels like to have your world turned upside down and your dreams crushed, to be headed down a path toward the future you've long planned—and find yourself knocked completely off that path.

This isn't the way I planned it, I thought to myself as I reached for my third box of tissues, my eyes red, nose stuffy, and face puffy. I stood bent over the kitchen counter, sobbing in desperation. So used to feeling in control of my life, I was suddenly and completely *not* in control.

This can't be happening to me, I thought. *This can't be the end.* But in my spirit, I knew it was. As *that* reality sunk in, my sobs turned into wails—uncontrollable and loud. If you'd been in the room, you would have recognized the unmistakable sound of grief that accompanies death. In this case I was mourning the death of my marriage. Reality overwhelmed me in wave after wave of sadness and uncertainty. I felt betrayed and fearful.

I knew what I had to do. But when you find yourself lying on a bed of thorns, remaining as still as possible seems less painful than attempting to extricate yourself.

As I sunk into utter misery, I was suddenly consumed by the fear that I might be having some sort of breakdown. I needed someone to hear me, to validate my despair. I picked up the phone and called my mother. She knew what I was going through, but she had never heard me like this. I couldn't get any words out, just sobs and gasps for air.

"Valorie?" she said anxiously. "What's wrong? What happened?"

"I can't stop crying," I finally muttered. "I feel like I'm going crazy. I feel like I'm losing my mind."

If I expected commiseration and comfort, I was in for a surprise. However, I should have known that my mother—a woman who has recovered from serious physical, financial, and family setbacks—wouldn't let me wallow in my misery. Looking back now, the situation reminds me of a scene in one of those old black-and-white movies where a panicked woman (that would be me) starts sputtering nonsense, her words coming faster and faster until finally someone (that would be my mom) slaps her across the face to bring her back to reality.

"You're not going crazy!" she declared. "You're human and you're in pain. Life and death are in the power of the tongue. The enemy wants you to say you're losing your mind. *You're not.* Now go into the bathroom," she said firmly. "Wash your face, and then go take a walk. It's a pretty day outside. Call me when you come back."

My mother's jarring words rang with truth. After some deep breaths, I felt just a glimmer of hope—a sudden uplifting of my soul. Sometimes, a glimmer of hope is all you need to take that next step forward. That step, for me, was a simple declaration: "This will not destroy me. I believe God, and in the Word He says He is with me wherever I go. So I will walk through this fire, but it will not consume me. *It will not.* On the other side of this, I will be a better and stronger woman."

YOUR RECOVERY BEGINS TODAY

That day my mother reminded me of an important lesson—our first guiding principle for facing a setback: *"I will not feel sorry for myself."* I had been knocked out, but her words were my wake-up call. Of course, it wasn't the last time I cried, but I never again cried from that woe-is-me place. In that pivotal moment, I chose faith over fear.

Today I want to help you make the same choice and embark on your own road to a better tomorrow.

It may be hard to believe now, but I'm convinced that on the other side of your difficult circumstances, something *good* is waiting, something better than you've previously thought or imagined. But to find it, you'll have to surrender your will and allow God's strength and grace to guide you.

Hebrews 11:1 says, "Faith is the substance of things hoped for, the evidence of things not seen" (NKJV). This truth gives you something to fiercely cling to when a setback pushes a dream so far out of reach that you start to lose hope. To the outside world, your hope may seem delusional. But that's when faith is most critical. That's when you are called to believe in the things "not seen." That's when you must choose to trust God to give you the desires of your heart, in His timing—or to turn your desires toward something ultimately better.

God may restore everything you have lost—or He may open your eyes to a new life, one filled with greater purpose and fulfillment than you can imagine at this moment. Our definition of success often differs greatly from His. If you're willing to let God realign your life to match His definition of success, you'll be able to view your setback not as a disappointment or failure but as a positive part of His plan to mold you and shape you according to His perfect design.

TEMPERED BY TRIALS

Successfully recovering from a setback is not just about restoring the externals you may have lost—such as the job, the money, the physical ability, or the relationship—or just regaining your footing on the path to your goals. It also involves strengthening your inner resilience.

The essence of resilience is your ability to effectively navigate adversity and courageously face whatever life throws your way. Though you may be bruised and battered by challenges, your spirit still soars. In fact, you choose to believe that you can become a better, richer person because of your experience.

You may be familiar with tempered steel or tempered glass—elements made stronger by repeated exposure to heat and cold. The *Merriam-Webster Dictionary* cites one definition of *temper* as "to make stronger and more resilient through hardship."[1] This is the opportunity your current setback offers: to have your character strengthened by the heat of battle so you emerge not only victorious but also forever changed for the better.

You may feel as if you're just hanging on right now, trying to survive.

But I want you to do more than survive. My goal is to help you eventually *thrive*. So this book has two parallel goals: first, to help you rebuild the aspects of your external world that have crumbled, and second, to help you gain the tools you need to not only navigate current setbacks but also to deal effectively with future surprises—because we know that change is the one constant in life.

Despite our best plans, earnest preparation, and good intentions, the truth is we don't have as much control of our lives as we like to think we do. You will inevitably face other challenges in the future, so why not embrace the opportunity now to gain skills that will help you recover more quickly next time? If you can grow through this difficult season, expanding your character, faith, and wisdom, then the journey you are on right now may just be one of the most important turning points of your life.

The Journey Matters as Much as the Destination

A central theme in this book is embracing the process, not just the desti-nation. Please don't rush through each chapter in an effort to get answers. Instead, let the words speak to you, prompting insight and reflection, transformation and hope.

We'll begin the journey together, right where you are—in the ditch of uncertainty, reeling from whatever unexpected shift has taken place in your life. Then step by step, as the pages turn, I'll help you get your bear-ings, determine your next steps, and begin walking a path toward a posi-tive future.

The principles outlined in this book are rooted in solid biblical prin-ciples and proven research in the field of positive psychology. While tra-ditional psychology, especially since World War II, has focused primarily on fixing what's wrong with people (a crucially important endeavor), positive psychology focuses on what goes right with people. What is it that makes us happier? more resilient? more fulfilled? Recent discoveries in this area offer some compelling and extremely practical advice for how to navigate major life challenges and come out on the other side a happier and wiser person.

In my own graduate studies at the University of Pennsylvania, I was excited to discover that so much scientific research aligns with the ancient wisdom of the Bible. I used these strategies to navigate the unexpected turns in my own life; and in each chapter, I will give you practical steps to craft your personal comeback out of unwelcome circumstances, whether your challenge is in the area of finances, work, relationships, health—or has impacted multiple aspects of your life.

Each chapter includes further guidance in the form of coaching exercises to increase your confidence, help you draw on your strengths, and deliberately propel you toward progress. Please don't skip these exercises! Only through deliberate, thoughtful action will you generate real change in your perspective and your circumstances.

In addition, all along the way you'll be inspired by real-life stories of resilience. You'll hear from people who have been paralyzed, lost their jobs, been forced into bankruptcy, endured painful divorces, lost their homes and hundreds of thousands of dollars, endured the death of a spouse or child or both—and yet somehow not only survived but eventually thrived. They were able to move forward—and to discover the fulfilling life God had planned for them.

As I spoke with these individuals who have endured so much with tenacity and faith, I gained perspective on my own setback. In fact, I began to view my own experience less as a setback and more as an opportunity to learn and grow. I realized that my life experience had taken me to emotional and spiritual depths I would never have reached otherwise. Would I have chosen to go through it? No. Am I a better person because I persevered and bounced back? Absolutely.

My sincere hope is that, one day, you'll be able to look back and say the same of your own experience. I'm planting the seed of hope because I know this to be true: "All things work together for good to those who love God, to those who are the called according to *His* purpose" (Romans 8:28, NKJV).

Don't try to figure out how it's going to "work together" just yet. Simply believe that it will and let God guide you forward, step by step.

The Five Commitments

When life blindsides you, it feels like you've been knocked off your path and into a ditch. What determines whether you stay in the ditch or climb out is how you choose to *think* about your circumstances while you are going through them. To climb out of the ditch and step onto a level path, you need to come to an agreement with yourself, to make a personal commitment that will transform your thinking and, ultimately, your life.

So as we begin this journey together, I ask you to commit to five simple rules about your thinking. No matter what your circumstances, the Five Commitments will serve as guiding principles for every step of your recovery, preventing you from straying onto paths of doubt or despair.

Commitment 1: I Will Not Feel Sorry for Myself

For a person who has suffered a setback, few things are more debilitating than self-pity. Feeling sorry for yourself makes you a victim rather than a victor. Worse, self-pity gives you an excuse to stay right where you are—to let regret and fear hold you hostage. Certainly there is a time to be sad and a time to mourn; these are appropriate, healthy responses to a setback. But there is no time to wallow.

Commitment 2: I Will Not Stare at the Closed Door

Letting go of the past is a necessary precursor to moving forward. It is tempting to think fondly of what used to be—to believe that life cannot be fulfilling or worthwhile without that relationship, that job, that role, that measure of success you've now lost. If you are so focused on staring at the closed door that you refuse to face forward, you'll never discover the open doors that lie ahead.

Commitment 3: I Will Dig Deep to Unearth All the Courage I Need

Without courage, a person knocked off course and into a ditch will stay there. Being afraid of making a wrong move, getting hurt, being embarrassed, or facing the future will paralyze you from taking action. The comeback process requires you to muster a great deal of courage. You need courage to believe better days are ahead. You need courage to ask for help. You need courage to let go of the past and deal with the uncertainty of the future. You need courage to start over—to take steps forward despite your fears. You may want to post 1 Corinthians 16:13 somewhere you'll see it often: "Be on your guard; stand firm in the faith; be courageous; be strong."

Commitment 4: I Will Direct My Thoughts—My Thoughts Will Not Direct Me

The difference between those who come back strong and those who wither is how they think—or, more precisely, how well they are able to manage self-sabotaging thoughts. Later we'll look more closely at the significant ways your thoughts influence your mood, motivation, and actions. For now, keep in mind this key principle: resilient people choose to think differently. They *believe* they can bounce back, and that belief leads them to take positive action toward their recovery.

Commitment 5: I Will Choose to Believe All Things Work Together for Good

In the midst of a storm, it can be hard to believe anything good will come. But it will. Sometimes it takes years to see what God is doing in a particular situation, but with patience, time, and faith, the good becomes more obvious. Choosing to believe that God is orchestrating the final outcome for good can provide the motivation you need to persevere in the face of overwhelming odds.

Read through the Five Commitments once more, and then make them part of your own personal comeback plan. To signify your commitment, photocopy the section below, then sign it to establish your pact with yourself. Post this contract wherever it will serve as a daily reminder of your choice to move forward.

MY PERSONAL COMMITMENTS

By signing below, I choose to live by the Five Commitments as part of my plan to recover from my setback and step onto the path to something better.

1. I will not feel sorry for myself.
2. I will not stare at the closed door.
3. I will dig deep to unearth all the courage I need.
4. I will direct my thoughts—my thoughts will not direct me.
5. I will choose to believe all things work together for good.

_____

Name

_____

Date

TWO

Where in the World Are You?

*How to Assess the Damage and Get Clear
About Exactly Where You Are*

O ne rainy summer afternoon in Atlanta several years ago, my travel
plans for the day took an unexpected turn. I
was in the right lane of a major street when
the eighteen-wheeler on my left decided to
make a right turn from the middle lane. As
the rig turned across my lane and the trailer
followed, I hit my brakes, but it was immediately obvious that no amount of braking
could prevent the inevitable. The collision
occurred in an instant, but I watched events
unfold in slow motion as my economy-sized
car was knocked completely off the road—
and landed in a ditch.

If you've ever been in a serious accident,
you know the feeling of disorientation that

- *Don't panic.
  Remain calm.*

- *Assess the damage
  realistically.*

- *Make a decision to
  get up rather than
  give up.*

takes over when the chaos stops. You are consumed by two questions: What just happened? and Is everybody okay?

As I sat trying to figure out the answer to those two questions, I gradually noticed the distinct sensation that my feet were wet. I looked down to see water from the ditch rising through the floorboards. To make matters worse, my car door was jammed. Four people had run to the scene, having watched the entire accident from a nearby gas station. They stared helplessly from the edge of the ditch, because the water ran too deep for them to reach me.

Though panic seemed a valid option at that point, I was determined to remain calm and wait for help. Eventually, an ambulance and fire trucks arrived. A fireman came to the rescue and literally lifted me out of the car. It was surreal and I was still a bit dazed, but also grateful for the number of strangers who had come to my aid in such a short period of time.

Sometimes life is like that. You're cruising along, thinking about the next goal on your journey, when you collide with a forty-ton truck of ugly reality and spin off into a ditch. Maybe you've recently been sent into a tailspin by financial challenges or relationship woes. Perhaps you or a loved one is facing a health setback that has threatened your dreams. Or maybe a job loss or business failure has left you asking, What just happened here?

Whatever the case, when you get knocked off course by life's unexpected challenges, your first task is not to assign blame or to ask, Why me? No matter who's at fault, the bottom line remains the same: you won't be getting to your intended destination—at least not as soon as you expected.

So what should you do? Your immediate priority is to get your bearings and assess the damage.

TAKE A DEEP BREATH

If life has just thrown you into a ditch, the first thing you need is not a road map. A basic truth of first aid is that moving around when you're disoriented, ill equipped, or injured can cause more damage than good. The impact of landing has probably left you feeling dizzy. You may have been knocked out only to wake up seeing stars and wondering, *Where in the world am I?* At this point your primary objective is not to figure out where you're going. It's to stabilize yourself, giving yourself a moment to get your bearings.

Resilience is not about having the right answers right away. In fact, some of the most resilient people are also among the most patient. They are patient with the process of change and patient with themselves.

Of course, patience doesn't feel like a natural priority when you find yourself knocked into the ditch of crisis. So here's what I'd like to ask you to do…

Breathe.

Life may not be what you hoped it would be right now, but you're still here. And there is a reason you're here. I know you wouldn't have planned it this way, but you cannot see the whole picture. God can. If you trust God, you know His will is to give you hope and a future (Jeremiah 29:11). The method He chooses may not make sense. It may not even seem fair, but I urge you not to spend your energy at this point trying to figure out your next step, because your spirit may simply not be ready.

There is a time to mourn, a time to be sad, a time to heal. This is that time. If you don't give yourself this time, you are likely to make decisions and start moving in directions that you will later regret. The shock of unwelcome change tends to bring out your fears. Operating from a place of fear is detrimental to your well-being and your ability to bounce back.

In the dizzy stage, you may be tempted to grab on to something—anything—that will help you feel stable. If you've just suffered a relationship loss, such as a divorce, you may jump into another relationship too quickly. And because your judgment is impaired, it will likely be an unhealthy connection. Before you know it, you might end up in another ditch, even deeper than the first. If you've had a financial setback, you may find yourself tempted to take on more debt, borrow from places that will make matters worse, or take on jobs that are not in your best long-term interests. If the setback is health related, your dizzy state could lead to frantic choices that complicate your situation.

Take the time to acknowledge the hit you've taken, so you can approach this pivotal change in your life with calm and wisdom that will empower you to bounce back fully and more quickly.

So again, the first thing I want you to do is breathe. Take a moment to get your bearings. You are in a state of shock right now, and you need to take some precautions in caring for yourself. Just as if you'd been hit and thrown into a ditch, lying flat on your back with a concussion and a broken bone or two, treat yourself gently. Don't move. Just breathe. In some situations, this may be for a short period and, for others, it may be longer. The goal is to stop long enough so that you are no longer seeing stars and stumbling with each step, too dizzy from the jolt to see straight.

DON'T MINIMIZE YOUR CHALLENGES

I know you may be used to pushing through the hard stuff. Perhaps you're the type that forges ahead as though your challenges are no big deal. But when you hit a challenge that knocks you off course, *it is a big deal*. I'm not suggesting you magnify your difficulties, but don't minimize them either. Acting as if no damage has been done can cause grave and unnecessary harm to your recovery process. Minimizing is a form of denial, a coping mechanism that allows you to admit to the existence of the problem but not to acknowledge the depth of it. By telling yourself things are really not that bad, you are able to survive without being overwhelmed by the weight of the truth. But the longer you minimize, the higher the price you will eventually have to pay. Ignoring problems doesn't make them go away. In fact, sometimes the setbacks we face are a result of years of denying the truth and minimizing reality.

Acknowledging the truth gives you the opportunity to find solutions to the real problems you face. Unless you are dealing with truth, you are not addressing the real problem.

Nine-year-old Tommy was in the basement of his family's home when his curiosity got the better of him. Finding some matches, he decided to try lighting one and holding it to the day's newspaper, just to see what would happen. Of course, Tommy's parents had warned him not to play with matches, but this little experiment was no big deal, he told himself. *I'm just going to strike one match and hold it up to this one newspaper. The fire will be small and I'll put it out real quick. I just want to see what will happen.*

Well, you can imagine what happened next. The newspaper caught fire a little faster than he expected. He dropped it on the floor. Now, you and I are adults. If we dropped a burning newspaper on the floor, we'd stomp on it. We'd put the fire out. But what would you do if you were a nine-year-old boy who was doing something his mom had already warned him *not* to do? You guessed it. You'd *run*! Tommy panicked and hurried up the basement stairs. Then he walked into the living room to sit down with his mom and brother as though nothing had happened!

A few minutes later his brother wrinkled his nose, sniffed the air, and asked, "Do y'all smell something? Smells like smoke."

Tommy looked around as though perplexed by the question. "No, I don't smell anything."

His mother did, though. And she roamed the house until she figured out where the smell was coming from. They called the fire department and she grabbed a fire extinguisher. The fire was still smoldering, but they were able to put it out before it caused much damage.

Tommy might have gotten away with his little indiscretion, but the singed tips of his shoestrings told the true story. His father noticed the evidence when he got home from work that day. Tommy got into big trouble, but he also learned an important lesson about the consequences of denying reality. The outcome could have been much worse.

What's the fire that is burning in your basement? In a panicked response to a scary turn in your life, you might try to convince yourself that eventually the problem will go away. But sooner or later, the smell of smoke will begin to impact other areas of your life.

John 8:32 says, "You will know the truth, and the truth will set you free." As you begin your journey out of the ditch, I challenge you to be truthful with yourself about the reality of the "fires" that are smoldering right now. If you ignore the weight of the truth, that fire can consume your entire house. You have time now to put the fire out before it grows larger—but only if you face it.

ASSESS THE DAMAGE REALISTICALLY

If you minimize the significance of what you are going through, it may work for the short term. Minimizing may help you temporarily avoid being overwhelmed by reality, and denial may allow you to keep intact the image you present to the world. But to navigate your way to authentic recovery, you must face the reality of what has happened so you can address it fully.

At the same time, you don't want to exaggerate the magnitude of your problem. Doing so can cause you to overreact, miss the opportunity for real answers, and deny the sovereignty of God in your situation.

Your goal should be to have the courage to assess the damage realistically. If you fail to accurately assess your situation—either panicking in fear or minimizing reality—you'll come up with solutions that will only waste your energy and resources at a time when you need them most.

When Vicky hit a major financial setback, she minimized the significance of the problem. A deep-seated fear of not having enough had plagued her since childhood. Some people deal with a fear of living in lack by overreacting to the slightest threat to their economic stability. They may work two or three jobs, or overwork at one job. They live so frugally they never enjoy the fruits of their labor. They become stingy and resent giving.

Others with a fear of lack take the opposite approach. When money challenges arise, they continue to spend as though nothing has changed. Sometimes, in an attempt to reduce their anxiety, they may spend more than usual, racking up credit card debt and ignoring warning signs. This was Vicky's approach.

When business began to slow down due to changes in the market, she was unrealistically optimistic about the prospects of new business. Cloaked in her favorite mantra, "You gotta have faith," she ignored the warnings that it was time to tighten the money belt and find new sources of revenue to supplement her income. Minimizing would have been okay if Vicky's problems had been short term, but when an underlying problem is driving you toward serious consequences, truth telling is crucial to your future recovery.

If you had observed Vicky's behavior, you would have seen the train wreck coming and called out to warn her: "Don't buy that! Save more. Spend less." But it wouldn't have mattered. Vicky was headed straight for an ugly collision with reality, and nothing could persuade her to change course. For two years she refused to face the truth about her growing debt. The thought of not having enough was too overwhelming. It didn't fit with her image of what her life should look like.

Then the payment on her adjustable rate mortgage rose 20 percent—and Vicky was undeniably in a ditch. With maxed-out credit cards, a credit line she was struggling to pay off, business down 40 percent, and barely enough income to pay herself, she was faced with the possibility of foreclosure—and the inescapable truth. While sitting at her kitchen table reading the letter from the bank threatening foreclosure proceedings, she finally heard her wake-up call. *They could take my house,* she realized. *I can't let that happen.*

The first step is admitting the truth. Rather than minimizing or exaggerating your circumstances, acknowledge them. Only by honestly assessing the damage can you choose a course of action to deal with it adequately. Sometimes, this can mean being open to another person's assessment of the damage.

Five weeks after my mother suffered a massive brain aneurysm that left her seriously physically disabled, I met with the medical team in charge of her care. She was out of the ICU and in rehabilitation, and the staff wanted to make sure her family understood the seriousness of the needs she would have after being released from the hospital. I had not yet visualized the massive change that was about to take place. At this point, my mother could not walk at all, had to be fed through a tube in her stomach because her swallowing muscles were not functioning, needed catheterization every few hours, and she could no longer see well, among other challenges. It became clear to the doctor that I had not thought through the details of how to manage her needs after she came home and family members were no longer in town to help.

"Life as you've known it with your mother is about to change drastically," the doctor said slowly, to give me time to process her words. "You need a plan." Her tone shook me. The reality scared me. But it also caused me to look at the truth: Mom would no longer have doctors and nurses 24/7. I would be responsible for her care. She couldn't be left alone for more than three or four hours at a time. I was so sad that my forty-nine-year-old mother was suffering like this, but instead of wallowing in grief over her loss of health and mobility, it was time for me to prepare for the new reality.

Certainly, the truth can hurt deeply. But part of your job is having the faith to believe that God can heal you where you hurt. Your pain and discomfort is not permanent, but unfortunately there may be no way around it. If you spend your time and energy either ignoring the fire in the basement or exaggerating the seriousness of your situation, your way out of the ditch will be longer and harder than it needs to be—you may even step onto the wrong path or begin moving in the wrong direction, all because you lack clarity. Think of the Israelites. Their eleven-day journey turned into a forty-year trek because their skewed perspective—exaggerating their suffering and minimizing their mistakes—stalled their progress.

When you go through a major shift in life, one of your greatest assets is the ability to see the truth clearly. To assess the damage you've suffered, you need to be able to see it for what it is. When you have clarity, you can make decisions that empower you to move forward with purpose and vision.

CHOOSE RESILIENCE

Once you've taken a deep breath and assessed the reality of your situation, you face a decision—one that carries crucial consequences for your future: Will you get up? Or will you give up? Will you be resilient or crack under pressure?

I know what you're going through is challenging, but the choice of how to respond is up to you. Getting up out of the ditch means taking control of what you can control, having the patience to persevere even when things seem to be moving slowly, and choosing an attitude that defines success realistically.

Get Up...or Give Up?

Ken and Carol had been co-workers in the public relations department of a Fortune 500 company for six years when they learned one Friday afternoon that both of their positions had been eliminated in a third round of layoffs. Many of their friends in the industry had also lost their jobs in the past few months, so they knew the competition for job openings was fierce and landing new positions would be that much more difficult.

Even so, Ken was optimistic from the start. Knowing the company had already let some people go, Ken had emotionally braced himself for the possibility of a layoff. He was upset when the news came through, but he didn't take it personally. He stopped by the offices of co-workers and key leaders he'd worked with to say good-bye, making the same request of each person, "You know, like I do, that it's tight in the job market these days and I'd like to land another position in public relations as quickly as I can. Can you think of anyone outside the company I should talk to as I look for my next job?" He received four leads.

That first Monday at home, reality hit hard. *I can't believe I'm unemployed,* he thought. Instead of giving in to discouragement, however, Ken got organized, created a plan of action that involved meeting with people, getting more involved in professional associations, landing a couple of freelance assignments, cutting back on expenses, and searching and applying for open positions daily. It took almost three months, but Ken landed another position in his field. He bounced back.

By contrast, Carol, who was actually more gifted at her job than Ken, felt pessimistic about her prospects after the layoff. She was competent in her work, but she viewed herself as inferior to her colleagues because she didn't hold a degree in communications or journalism. In fact, she had started at the company as a sales assistant and worked her way into the public relations department, a feat that underscored her communications skills. But Carol didn't see it that way. She attributed her success to luck and a kind departmental manager who had chosen to give her a break.

When the layoff came, her first thought was that, given her lack of a degree, she'd have to go back into sales support, something she no longer wanted to do. She also took the news personally. "I worked so hard, yet my efforts didn't matter in the end," she commented repeatedly. "Maybe I'm just not as good as I thought I was."

During the first couple of weeks after the layoff, Carol was down in the dumps. Many days she couldn't get herself organized enough to write cover letters and send out resumes to the appropriate people. She spent a lot of time feeling sorry for herself as she thought about how great her job had been and entertained the likelihood that she would not find another situation like that. And how would she explain why *she* was one of the people laid off? Surely, a prospective employer would think she must have been at least somewhat to blame. Carol's discouragement deepened as she thought about all the people with more experience and education who were also looking for jobs in her chosen field. She didn't reach out to former colleagues. She had not become active in local professional associations, so she didn't have any industry contacts outside of those from her former company. She put in a few resumes on job sites that were hiring in the public relations field, but when she didn't hear back after a week or so, she decided to look for sales support positions.

After eight months, she found a job in the sales division of a reputable company. It wasn't what she wanted. Carol went backward rather than forward. But why? The truth is, Carol never really believed she could have what she wanted. For much of her time in public relations, she'd felt like an imposter, as if she was doing something she really didn't have the credentials to do. So she didn't put much effort into landing a position in her preferred field. After all, if it was all just a fluke that she'd landed her previous job, what was the likelihood she'd end up so lucky again?

—— *Resilient People Know. . .* ——

Resilience is a skill that can be honed. The more you practice it, the better you get.

It's All in Your Mind

The disparity between Ken's and Carol's experiences is typical of many situations. Two people are knocked down by a similar adversity. One gets up. The other gives up. It isn't talent or random luck that determines the outcome.

Resilient people think differently.

According to psychology researchers, the major difference between those who bounce back and those who don't is their *thinking style*. It's about how you interpret the things that happen to you and how you choose to respond to them.

Ken and Carol approached the same setback from different perspectives. In the face of adversity, both were disappointed and concerned about their futures. Carol did not believe in herself, even though she was the more talented of the two. She also interpreted the layoff as a personal failure, rather than recognizing that economic factors were solely to blame. Ken, on the other hand, saw the reasons for his job loss as completely external. The company was struggling. Ken knew that certain departments—accounting, for example—were more resistant to layoffs because they were essential to the running of the company. In his mind, this was just the nature of the business climate and had absolutely nothing to do with him. Ken believed in himself and in his ability to land another job in his field. As a result, his actions led him to achieve his goal.

Ken did something else that was critical to his comeback: he reached out to others. Rather than isolating himself, he intentionally sought assistance—meeting with people, going to professional meetings, asking colleagues to help him in his job search. And they did.

When faced with a major setback, you can choose to push through it, learn lessons from it, and never give up—or you can choose to be helpless, defeated, and stuck. Dr. Karen Reivich, one of the foremost researchers in the field of resilience, observed, "It's your thinking style that determines your level of resilience—your ability to overcome, steer through, and bounce back when adversity strikes."[1]

Resilience is not about restoring the external things you've lost—whether a job, money, home, relationships, or physical abilities. It is about developing your ability to withstand whatever adversities come your way—the fortitude to weather life's inevitable storms with your faith and courage intact. So bouncing back is largely an internal skill, one that requires a strong, positive attitude.

Today I invite you to make that crucial decision. Will you get up or give up?

You Have Everything You Need

Use the Power of Your *Thoughts*

Today, notice your thinking style. Are you being pessimistic or optimistic? In what ways are you internalizing your setback? What would be a healthier way of looking at your circumstances?

Use the Power of Your *Words*

Say it out loud: "I have the resilience to handle this setback. I will rise to the challenge."

Use the Power of Your *Actions*

Identify one step you can take in the direction of bouncing back. It doesn't have to be large or difficult. You build momentum one step at a time. Sometimes a small step is the most important.

Use the Power of *Relationships*

Who do you want to connect with today? It can be as simple as sharing a loving moment, expressing a kind word, or sharing your declaration about bouncing back with a positive person in your life. Positive connection with others energizes you.

Use the Power of *Prayer*

Lord, I believe You are the source of my ability to be resilient. I pray that I will be strengthened for this journey. Give me the resolve and determination to push through the thoughts and fears that threaten to hold me back. Amen.

Triumph Over Trials: Kevin's Story

When I was in high school, one of the best distance runners in the state of Colorado was my classmate Kevin Wolitzky. He was all-state in three sports—track, cross-country, and baseball. Upon graduation he won a full athletic scholarship to play baseball at the University of Northern Colorado (UNC). But his dreams of coaching baseball, maybe even playing professionally, were cut short soon after he arrived.

As newcomers to the UNC baseball team, Kevin and his fellow freshman teammates took part in a hazing ritual in October 1990 that involved sliding head first into a mud puddle out in right field and then competing in a mud wrestling match. In a freak accident, Kevin slid into the mud puddle and hit his head at a dangerous angle. The result was devastating—a spinal cord injury to the fifth and sixth cervical vertebrae.

Kevin was paralyzed from the neck down.

I recall visiting Kevin in the hospital, along with about fifteen of our mutual friends, during Thanksgiving break in 1990. His spirits were high. He smiled at us and even cracked a few jokes, despite the metal screws in his skull that held the halo in place above his head. I'd been in awe of his discipline as an athlete, and now I was in awe of his attitude in the hospital.

The next time I saw Kevin was ten years later at our high school reunion. He smiled and snapped his fingers as he joined a group of us on the dance floor. He had a lot to be smiling about—he was newly engaged. I discovered that not only had he returned to UNC in the fall of 1991, just a year after his accident, but he had also finished his degree in physics five years later and went on to work for Hughes Aircraft.

You might expect me to tell you Kevin had a miraculous recovery from his paralysis. He didn't. Kevin is still a quadriplegic. But it hasn't stopped him from living out many of the dreams he had as a teenager. Now married with three little girls, Kevin drives himself to work at the job he's held since 1996. He met his wife, Leda, at work, and he calls her his "angel." She turned out to be the unselfish woman whose love was big enough to embrace Kevin's unique challenges.

Without a trace of bitterness, Kevin recently recounted for me what the years following his injury have been like. "I've gotten to do most of the things I wanted to do, the major things," he says, referring to his career, marriage, and children. "I'm really thankful for that. For me, the only part I didn't plan was my accident. Just about everybody can say, 'This isn't how I planned it.'"

And Kevin is right: if you live long enough, you'll have the experience of being knocked into a ditch. But Kevin's ditch was deeper than most. There was no going back to the way life used to be. His new path definitely required a steeper climb than the one he had planned—which makes his attitude all the more profoundly inspiring.

"I believed I could still live a full life, full of all the things that God lets us experience—some painful, some joyful," he told me. "I didn't see the challenges as much as others did. I just knew there were other quadriplegics who have been successful and I could be too." Was he afraid? Yes. After five months in the hospital, Kevin was scared when he got home. In the hospital, a nurse or doctor was just a call button away, but at home, he was faced with the magnitude of his physical challenges.

Even so, he focused on getting himself ready to go back to school that fall. And he even found something for which to be thankful: As a baseball player, he wouldn't have had time for the demands of a physics degree. But now he could pursue the physics major while minoring in mathematics and environmental science. "I went back to school because I wanted to prove to myself I could do it. Now my degree allows me to work in a technical job and provide for my family."

Still, stepping into his new life—a life so unexpected and unwelcome—was a struggle. "I went through the grief, the anger, the devastation, the frustration, the pain. You go through all these different stages," he remembers. "I used to cry every time I woke up. I realized this is not going away. Then I would cry every night going to bed because someone had to help me. Then it was every other night, then once a week, then once a month. Now, it just creeps up on me every once in a while."

What stands out most about Kevin is how strongly he *believed* he could still pursue the life he imagined for himself. I asked where that belief came from. He paused for a long time before giving me his answer: "That's a tough one—I think maybe it is a divine gift." He also mentioned something else, something he developed long before the accident: discipline. "I knew what it took to run under a five-minute mile. The drive is the same. God put something in us that gives us the ability to persist and that leads to winning, not just against someone else but for yourself. All of that discipline helped me to never give up. It helped me to cope... Who you are before your setback is really going to shape who you are after."

Kevin, who with the help of others has even gone water-skiing and snow skiing, has a vision for his next twenty years. "I want to see my children graduate from high school. If they choose college or a vocation, I want to see that. I want to see them get married. My vision has gone from all the things I wanted to do, to all the things I want to see. Having a vision is transforming."

Bouncing back from a setback, for Kevin, didn't mean getting back all of the physical abilities he'd lost. It meant persevering and living fully despite that loss. "I have had frustration and a little jealousy," he admits, "of fathers that pick up their kids and throw them around and catch them, or play baseball and soccer. That is a bummer. But I can only control what I can control."

Sometimes, that is our destiny: learning how to move forward despite the injuries we sustained when we landed in that ditch. It requires getting used to a new normal. The victory comes in accepting what we cannot control, controlling what we can, and glorifying God in how we live our lives.[2]

KEVIN'S LESSONS FROM THE DITCH

- *The only one you ever have to glorify is God.* Make sure He gets the glory from your trials.

- *You can become a better person as a result of your setbacks.* Allow your challenges to give you a better perspective on what's important—your family, your friends, and your salvation.

- *Don't suppress your emotions.* Honor them. Grieve your loss so you can move forward. It will take time, but your recovery will take much longer if you pretend these emotions aren't there.

- *You have to rebuild with patience.* Do one thing. And then do another. Build on the first step, then take another step. When I got knocked off my path, I said, "First, let me learn to feed myself one meal, then maybe tomorrow, I can feed myself two meals." Persistence is probably one of the greatest traits you can hone or develop.

- *Find something consistent to create some sense of stability.* When you are disoriented and you stand up in that ditch, you need to find something you can focus on and rely on. It might be a family member or a friend you can always count on for prayer or a support group of some sort.

- *Humble yourself to accept help.* And when you need it but no one offers, ask. You must let go of thinking you have to do everything yourself.

How Did You End Up Here?

Examining the Path That Led You Here Can Yield Crucial Clues About What to Do—and What Not to Do—Next

- *Look for the lessons.*

- *Don't make any hasty decisions.*

- *Ask the right questions and answer them honestly.*

- *Stop asking yourself, Why me?*

Claire had always had it together. Known to her friends as Superwoman, she raised three bright, healthy children, mostly on her own. She was a rock in her family, the one everyone else called when they needed help. She loved the Lord. And her career was stellar: twenty years of steadily climbing the corporate ladder as a media sales executive. But her world started unraveling a few years ago.

First, her boss began making unwelcome advances. When Claire rebuffed him, she lost her job—and the accompanying six-figure salary. She filed a sexual harassment complaint, but it was clear she needed to find employment elsewhere.

Claire soon landed in a new career in real

estate—just before the mortgage market took a tremendous hit. So once again, she found herself seeking work; this time competing with a huge pool of applicants for every potential position. The one bright spot amid the multiple challenges was her developing relationship with a brilliant business owner she'd met during her dealings in the real estate industry. They dated long distance and quickly fell in love. He soon proposed, and when she said yes, he was eager to make it official with a ceremony.

"I didn't see any reason to get married right away," Claire says, "but he kept asking me to reconsider, so I finally said okay." Claire married him and moved her three teenagers from North Carolina to California. She'd expected the marriage to bring the love and companionship she'd waited so many years to find. "The entire time we were dating, he did all the right things and said all the right things," Claire remembers.

In retrospect, she realizes that a longer courtship might have revealed the real man. The truth is, she wasn't in the right place to make such a life-changing decision: in less than a year, she'd lost two jobs, gotten married, and moved. She thought her problems were at an end; in reality, they were just beginning.

The ongoing turmoil in the real estate market soon caused her new husband's business to falter. She worked frantically alongside him to keep the company afloat, to no avail. In just three months, they ran through all of their savings—nearly a half million dollars—trying to keep the business going and employees paid. When they finally were forced to shut down, Claire looked for and found consulting work back home in North Carolina—and they all moved, *again*. Then her husband fell into a deep depression. For weeks at a time, he would not leave the bedroom. He refused to pray or exercise, both of which they usually did together daily. His behavior became unpredictable and irrational.

Even as her husband's emotional health deteriorated, Claire's mother was diagnosed with ALS, commonly known as Lou Gehrig's disease. A sibling who had suffered a brain injury lived at home with her mother, but since he wasn't able to provide the care required, Claire would still need to check on her mother multiple times each day.

Now earning less than a third of her previous salary, Claire was carrying the weight of supporting the entire family—not just her spouse and children but also her mother and brother. The move south meant the cost of living was more reasonable, but it was still a strain. Her mother's medications alone cost nine hundred dollars per month. Daily, an exhausted Claire got up early enough to drive thirty miles to her mother's home so she could feed her, then she went to work; at lunchtime she drove back to her mother's, then to work again, then back to her mother's after work to feed her dinner and care for her other needs. Then Claire would drive home thirty miles to a spouse who was still in bed. She'd make dinner, spend some time with the kids, go to bed, and do it all over again the next day.

"One day," she recalls, "I was in the kitchen, and I just fell to my knees." She prayed, *"Lord, how much more? Why would You bring someone into my life I thought was my soul mate and that person isn't here for me emotionally during the most trying time of my life? He won't even go see my mother even though she asks about him every day."*

Here's how she describes God's response: *"You cannot expect him to give you what he does not have to give. Remember that I am here with you and I am all you need."*

Claire says it was as if a light bulb turned on. She realized she couldn't rely on her own understanding about why things were happening the way they were, but she was sure of one thing: God was with her.

She would need Him even more in the months to come. Just a few weeks after her light-bulb moment with the Lord, Claire's husband left to pursue a work opportunity in another city. He never came back or called. Two months later Claire's mother died.

Through this long and difficult season, two things contributed greatly to Claire's eventual comeback: her faith grew stronger in the face of her challenges, and she determined not to be bitter but to grow better as a result of her trials.

LOOK FOR THE LESSONS

As I've coached clients and interviewed people about their experiences of getting knocked off course, I've realized that setbacks are rarely isolated. Like a falling domino that sets in motion everything else in its path, a health challenge often leads to a job loss which leads to financial trouble which leads to a foreclosure and a lifestyle change and maybe even relationship trouble.

So navigating setbacks often means navigating multiple issues at once. And yet, as Claire discovered, if God is the source of your stability, you will have the strength to make it through.

But surely you want to do more than just survive. If you don't learn something from your experience, what's to keep you from ending up in a similar situation in the future? So it's wise to reflect on how you ended up here—not for the purpose of beating yourself up over any mistakes or regrettable decisions, but for the purpose of learning the lessons God offers during the biggest challenges we face.

As Claire reviews the jarring twists her life has taken over the past few years, she notes, "Some decisions I made were ones I would not have made at other times in my life." She realizes now that the job setbacks and her mother's illness had put her in a vulnerable state of mind, which led to some poor decisions. If she had not been in that state, she might have insisted on a longer engagement, which may have given her time to see cracks in the relationship. Or she might not have moved her family but convinced her husband to find a way to move to them.

Not every setback can or should be attributed to our own decisions, but certainly challenges can be made worse by our poor choices. It is liberating and wise to admit when our own actions have compounded the effects of a setback. By telling yourself the truth, you are set free from repeating your mistakes. By noticing the reasons you made a mistake, you can be on the alert when similar circumstances present themselves in the future.

Take a look at a few of the lessons Claire says she learned:

- *Listen to that voice inside.* "It's God speaking to you! There was a little voice that said, *'Don't take that job in North Carolina.'* There was a voice that said, *'Don't marry him right away. Wait a few months.'* Over and over, that voice said, *'You know better. Don't do it.'* And I didn't listen. Maybe if I'd listened to that voice, I would have discovered the information I needed that would have prevented me from marrying the wrong person."

- *Don't get ahead of God.* "I prayed about getting married and God didn't answer, so I decided to move ahead on my own." She learned that being out of God's perfect will is not a place she wants to be again.

- *Don't let others pressure you into a decision.* "I didn't want to move to California, but my husband got the kids excited and on board, so I just gave in." Again, she put his judgment ahead of her own intuition.

CONSIDER YOUR NEXT MOVE CAREFULLY

Of course, the lessons you can learn from your present circumstances don't apply only to future, unrelated setbacks—in fact, they may very well have a direct bearing on the choices you make in your current situation. By learning your lessons now, you will be better equipped to get the help you need. You will have sharper discernment about how to move forward and who to call (or not call) on for help.

Keep in mind what we learned in the previous chapter. When you wake up in a ditch, your first impulse is to climb out as quickly as possible. But the truth is, you need to fully assess the damage and get a clear perspective on the situation before you make a move. You need to know whether you'll be jumping from a crashed car to safety—or into a flooded ditch of rushing muddy water!

If you're committed to long-term resilience, you'll determine to learn a few lessons before you even attempt to find your way back to the path that leads to your goal. In fact, in learning the lessons, you may determine you don't even want to get back on the same path you were on anyway.

If you are the type of person who tends to be in a hurry, this is a particularly important point to remember. Often when faced with a setback, you'll be tempted to make quick or easy decisions to propel yourself beyond the immediate situation. Problem is, those same decisions may steer you onto a path you later have no desire to walk. You need to be aware that midcrisis is not the right time to make major decisions.

Caitlin had been employed with her company for seventeen years. She had just bought a new car, and her adjustable-rate mortgage was about to go higher, but she wasn't worried because she was expecting a pay raise. Instead, cutbacks at work led to furloughs and a salary cut. In the first few months, Caitlin covered her increased costs by dipping into her savings. When her savings cushion ran out, she paid for groceries, gas, and other expenses with her credit cards, but she didn't pay the balances at the end of each month. Soon her cards were nearly maxed out. She searched for a new job but couldn't even land an interview.

For quite a while, her boyfriend had been pushing the idea of marriage, but Caitlin had some concerns about their relationship and so had resisted taking that step. As her financial situation worsened, she began to reconsider. She rationalized that the red flags that had given her pause merely reflected her doubts about marriage in general; in doing so, she ignored the warning signs that were telling her to slow down this relationship.

Before long, she'd talked herself into getting married. Her boyfriend was elated.

They married three months later, and Caitlin's financial pressures dissolved almost immediately when he moved from his apartment to her home and they shared the expenses. Her temporary financial woes were solved. But her marriage was permanent—and it carried a whole different set of issues. With her vision no longer clouded by the stress of figuring out how to pay bills, the red flags she'd seen so clearly before her financial troubles began were suddenly unmistakable again.

The good news is that, with counseling and a lot of patience, she and her husband worked through their problems. But it wasn't easy, and it would have been much wiser to work through the issues prior to marriage. Caitlin says if she could do it over again, she would not have gotten married when she did. She'd make her decision to marry—or not—based on heartfelt, divinely guided certainty rather than caving to financial uncertainty.

Claire's and Caitlin's stories both underscore the dangers of making a difficult situation even worse through poor decisions. Here are a few of the common ways that people sabotage their comeback after waking up in a ditch:

- rekindle or start doomed relationships
- make poor financial choices, such as spending carelessly or draining a savings account
- stop taking care of themselves; for example, by not exercising or eating well

- resist seeking the help of others to bounce back
- make permanent decisions based on temporary circumstances

Don't sabotage yourself. When you recognize you are being illogical or unhealthy, put the brakes on. It takes discipline to make hard choices and change course, but you will be better off for it.

One of the most important steps you can take is to honestly examine the path that brought you to this point. If choices within your control contributed to your setback, take note. Learn from your mistakes so you don't repeat them.

HONEST ANSWERS TO TOUGH QUESTIONS

When life becomes painful enough, obvious questions begin to surface about the reasons behind the pain. When you were uncomfortable, but not miserably so, you could ignore those questions—or just give superficial answers.

How's your relationship? "Oh, it's good!" you exclaim without much thought.

How's your job? "Just fine" is your routine answer.

But there comes a point when you can't keep up the lies. Suddenly you realize that your responses are not authentic. And you start to wonder, *What's my real answer to these simple questions?* Perhaps the relationship is hanging by a thread. Or you dread getting out of bed to go to work. Or you are so far underwater financially, you feel you'll never see daylight again. To drill down to the underlying truth, ask yourself some tough questions:

- What truth are you afraid to acknowledge about your life right now?
- What are you afraid will happen if you admit the truth?

- What specific problem has you feeling stuck?
- What is the most frustrating part of that for you?
- Do your fear and frustration say something about your role in why you've landed in this situation? If so, what does it say?
- What needs to change in order for you to accept reality— and to begin to deal with it?

Mandy had long ignored her doctor's warning that she needed to start exercising more and cut back on her high-fat, traditional Southern diet. For years, she glossed over internal questions like, *Should I really eat that?* and *How do I feel about myself?* "It's just two pieces of fried chicken," she rationalized. "I'm not *that* overweight," she convinced herself whenever she looked in the mirror. She brushed aside other questions as well. In response to the standard "How are you?" she always responded, "I'm feeling great"—ignoring the fact that she got winded climbing a single flight of stairs and seemed never to feel fully rested.

Then a heart attack at age fifty-three tossed her in the ditch. Waking up in the hospital following heart surgery made it rather difficult to deny her condition any longer. Given a second chance at life, now the truth stares her in the face. She can still choose not to adopt healthier habits, but she can no longer deny that her choices have consequences. It's time for Mandy to ask—and answer—some tough questions.

As her coach, I have asked Mandy, "Do you want to live? What is your reason for wanting to live? What are you willing to do to get healthy and when will you start? In what way(s) are you prone to sabotage your own success and who could hold you accountable to keep that from happening?"

What about you? What truths have you previously glossed over that are now glaringly obvious as you lie on your back in the ditch? What questions have you been dodging that are now unavoidable? This isn't about blaming yourself for your setback or beating yourself up for what you could have or should have done. It is about embracing the power of the truth to set you free and to light your way to a healthier, more authentic path.

Resilient People Know...

Never make an important decision in the heat of negative emotions; they impair your decision-making ability. Positive emotion—from laughter, a hug, or even a small bit of good news—can help you make thoughtful decisions. "The joy of the LORD is your strength" (Nehemiah 8:10).

Certainly, answering the question of how you ended up here can be painful, because it sometimes conjures up thoughts of what might have been—you might find yourself thinking, *If only I had...* Even when our setbacks have absolutely no relation to our own actions, we find ourselves tempted to spend too much time brooding on the *if onlys*. Perhaps a bad accident has left you with some health challenges. Refuse to get stuck imagining what would have happened "if only." Maybe you lost a loved one through no fault of your own and yet you are still having if-only thoughts. If that is you, please stop. I cannot say often or clearly enough that not all setbacks are a result of our harmful habits or bad choices, so do not take that undeserved weight of guilt on yourself. Instead invite God to make it clear what wisdom you are to glean from this experience as you move forward.

Whatever your circumstance, if-only thinking will just keep you stuck in the ditch. This is especially true when your setback could have been prevented by your own actions. If this is true of your situation, make a choice to forgive yourself so you can move on. Whether you were laid off and you think you could have done something to prevent it, or you landed in divorce court and think you should have made a better choice of spouse, remember that energy spent regretting past choices will slow your progress toward a resilient recovery. Instead, forgive yourself and free yourself to focus on moving forward—while determining to learn all you can from the experience.

THE ONE QUESTION TO AVOID

When people wake up in unfamiliar territory, bruised and confused, their most common question is, Why me?

Have you pondered this question, even for a moment? In the process of understanding how you ended up here, you may wonder, *Why has this happened to me? What have I done to deserve this? Have I done something wrong? Am I being punished? Is God angry with me? Do I just have bad luck?*

The string of negatively framed questions leads to counterproductive statements. "Things never go right for me." "Something is wrong with me." "Other people are obviously better/smarter/more blessed because they've been spared the trouble I'm dealing with."

Bottom line: Asking, Why me? is self-defeating. It will leave you feeling sorry for yourself or angry at God or others. Take another look at the first of the Five Commitments you made at the start of this book: "I will not feel sorry for myself." Instead, you want to focus on understanding the dynamics that led you to this place. And if any of those dynamics is within your control, don't you want to know that? If something is within your control, that means you can change it. Your setback may not fit into this category, but if it does, it is best to be aware early so you can shorten the amount of time required for you to bounce back and so you can prevent similar circumstances from recurring.

The key is to remember that setbacks are part of life. While we would like for it to proceed smoothly, with only our plans to contend with, life doesn't work that way. "In their hearts humans plan their course, but the LORD establishes their steps," Proverbs 16:9 promises. The true test of resilience is the ability to navigate the stuff we don't plan.

GO STRAIGHT TO THE SOURCE OF WISDOM

There is one definite benefit to being knocked off course: it forces us to stop. In our fast-paced culture, we rarely slow down long enough to ponder life. We continue traveling toward what we think is our goal without noticing the signposts along the way. If we're not careful, our choices become rote, habitual, hastily made, and poorly thought through. Years can go by without our deeply considering the effects of our choices.

So now, when life has crashed to a halt, you have a chance to pause, be honest with yourself, and pray for wisdom.

The Holy Spirit will guide you. Ask God to give you the courage to dig deep and the wisdom to answer the tough questions with fresh insight. Invite Him to open your eyes and heart so you can find your way onto your unique path. James 1:5 says, "If any of you lacks wisdom, you should ask God, who gives generously to all without finding fault, and it will be given to you."

So as you seek answers to how you ended up here and what you can learn from it, take a moment to open your heart to God's voice:

*Lord, I need wisdom right now. I don't expect all of the
answers today. But I am asking You to help me ask the right*

questions and to have the courage to answer them honestly. Help
me gain insight where I need it. Help me accept the things I cannot
change. And give me the clarity to see what things I can change
and the strength to change them.

CAPTURE THE LESSONS TODAY

I've learned that some of life's hard-earned lessons can get left behind if we don't capture them on paper right away. Once you climb out of the ditch, it's hard to remember exactly what it felt like at the bottom. Capture the message life is sending you right now so you can use these lessons later. Keep in mind, this isn't about beating yourself up but rather about deciding to learn all the lessons you can from your setback.

Please don't skip over these questions or any others in this book. I understand that they may highlight the frustration or pain or anger or fear you feel right now. But by taking the time to give voice to your feelings and to the insights you're gaining, I promise you will find clarity about where to go from here.

If you're uncomfortable putting your thoughts in this book, feel free to grab your private journal and work through the questions there.

What steps or events led you to this situation? Can you trace your setback to a specific decision or turning point?

Is there any aspect of your circumstance that was within your control to prevent or change? If so, what was it and what lesson have you learned about yourself that might shape your future decisions?

What aspects of your current circumstances resulted from things completely out of your control? How does this knowledge impact your view of the situation?

What lesson(s) and message(s) are being offered to you in your ditch?

What is that voice inside you trying to tell you right now?

Have you made (or are you tempted to make) any permanent decisions based on temporary challenges? If yes, what is the decision? Can you put a hold on that decision until you are in a more stable place in your life?

Are there any messages you've been ignoring that it is time to finally acknowledge?

You Have Everything You Need

Use the Power of Your *Thoughts*

When your life first gets thrown off course, don't rush to jump out of the ditch. Notice the dynamics that led you to the ditch. It is possible that the dynamics were totally beyond your control. Sometimes, though, you can identify personal choices that contributed to your current circumstances. Ask yourself, What lesson or message can I take away from this ditch?

Use the Power of Your *Words*

Finding the accurate answer to "How did I end up here?" takes wisdom. Meditate on these powerful words from James 1:5: "If any of you lacks wisdom, you should ask God, who gives generously to all without finding fault, and it will be given to you."

Use the Power of Your *Actions*

Let careful thought be your action. Be still and ponder.

Use the Power of *Relationships*

If you struggle with finding the lessons being offered to you, enlist the help of a trusted person to help you glean wisdom from your setback.

Use the Power of *Prayer*

God, I am grateful for Your grace. Thank You for the chance to learn lessons that will help me climb out of this ditch with something of value: wisdom gained. Show me what You want me to learn and how You want me to grow as a result of my current circumstances. Amen.

Triumph Over Trials: Deanna's Story

Sometimes you don't realize the significance of a setback until years later. Deanna Jones knows this all too well. As a child, Deanna's dream was to be a mother. But whenever an adult would ask, "What do you want to be when you grow up?" her answer seemed to disappoint them. "Oh, sweetheart, you can do so much more than that!" her aunt once said. "What do you want to *do*? You could be a pilot or a doctor or an actress. Don't you want to *do* something besides just be a mommy?" Eventually, the little girl came up with an answer that seemed to please the adults in her life: she would become a singer.

A talented young vocalist, Deanna landed a job shortly after high school singing at Disney World in a group called Kids of the Kingdom. By age nineteen, she had her own place, a boyfriend, and a singing career. Then she learned she was pregnant.

"I reverted back to what I was told as a child," she remembers. "You have to *be* somebody before you have a child." Even so, she says, "In my heart of hearts, I wanted to have the baby." She even named the baby Aubrey. But Deanna didn't listen to her heart. "Although I grew up in a spiritually solid home, the mentality of the people I was around at that time—far from home—was that it was no big deal. Just make the problem go away." That's just what Deanna did.

"From the minute my boyfriend dropped me off at the abortion clinic, I fell into a deep pit," she admits. "One day, I'm ten weeks pregnant and singing about dreams coming true. The next day, I'm having an abortion. Then, two days later, I'm back at Disney World singing in front of Cinderella's castle."

She tried to pretend she was happy—and for six months, she continued the charade. But as depression set in, Deanna eventually quit her job and moved to California with her boyfriend, hoping to escape the pain. She auditioned for several opportunities in Los Angeles, but truthfully, she simply didn't care about pursuing singing and fame anymore. She eventually broke up with the boyfriend too.

"I didn't want to live," she says. Finally she decided it was time to take her own life. "I was getting ready to take the pills when my mother called." Her mother didn't know about the abortion, although months earlier, her mother had told her of a dream she'd had that Deanna was pregnant but then had an abortion. Deanna had denied it, just as she pretended on this day that all was well. As she talked to her mother, she gave no hint that she was on the verge of killing herself. Nonetheless, the call saved her life. When she hung up the phone, she stared at the pills. She couldn't bring herself to go through with it. "I thought, *If I feel this awful after losing my child that I never even saw, I cannot imagine what this would do to my mother,*" Deanna remembers.

That's when she finally called on God. She laid her head on the carpet and cried out, "I don't know how to get out of this pit!" This simple confession was a pivotal moment. "Confession to the Lord was my lifeline," she explains. "It was the thing that initiated change overnight." She began to long to know who He was.

Her confession opened up a whole new way of thinking. "I no longer believed that motherhood is something you do after there are no other options. My perception changed. I accepted that my first dream, my *purest* dream, was to be a mother." Although she continued to sing and work in show business, she shifted her priorities, focusing on more important aspects of her life, such as having a relationship and eventually becoming a mom.

Several years later Deanna married. Her husband was only the second person she told about the abortion (the first being her former boyfriend). They had a daughter, Samantha. When Samantha was five, they took her to Florida. "It was my first time at Disney World since the time of the abortion. It was an amazing redemption!" Deanna says. "There I was with my daughter after having aborted a girl years earlier. The best surprise was that five weeks later, I learned that I had conceived another child while on vacation at Disney!"

When their two children, Samantha and Andrew, were older (twenty and fourteen, respectively), Deanna felt a strong call to adopt. She and her husband adopted baby Matea from Guatemala six years ago. Shortly after, she had a dream in which a pair of brown hands offered her an orange. The dream made sense a year later after they adopted three biological siblings from Ethiopia who had been orphaned: Grace, Ella, and Jared, now thirteen, ten, and nine. "Grace and I were talking, and I asked her what her Ethiopian nickname was," Deanna says. "She said her Ethiopian mother called her a name that in English means 'orange.' Ella chimed in and said, 'Yeah, she called me that, too!'"

Deanna's journey from the ditch to complete restoration took nearly a quarter century. The final chapter of healing began in 2007 when she started writing a book about motherhood. She wanted to encourage mothers and aspiring mothers, but she had no intention of mentioning the fact that, years ago, she had forsaken her first opportunity to be a mother.

"As I wrote the book, I realized that I couldn't write it without sharing my entire experience," she says. Deanna had not even told her mother. Now she would be telling the whole world. In writing through her regret and grief, she was finally able to forgive herself. "I felt it would invalidate the price Christ paid on the cross if I rejected God's forgiveness," she explains. Despite the fact that she still *felt* she didn't deserve forgiveness, she *made the decision* to forgive herself. "It was then that I was able to claim that daughter I'd had, and then to grieve her. I wailed and cried out of genuine grief." She went through a post-abortion recovery group.

Ironically, on December 17 of that year, in the midst of Deanna's grieving, her cousin had a baby girl named Aubrey Hope. The cousin had no knowledge of Deanna's abortion two decades earlier, but Aubrey was the same name Deanna had given her unborn daughter—the daughter who would have been born in mid-December.

Today, Deanna is an adoption advocate and author of the book *To Be a Mother*. She also sings with a big-band group. She has performed at the White House for President George W. Bush, at the wedding of Michael Douglas and Catherine Zeta-Jones, and at events for other celebrities. "As a young woman, I chose a path that said, 'I will be famous and make money so that I can pursue my first dream,' but the aftermath of the abortion made me realize I wanted to pursue my first dream first. I didn't want a pursuit of fame to get in the way of my first dream."

Deanna agrees strongly with Commitment #5; she sees in her journey clear evidence that all things work together for good. She learned that lesson two years ago as she fasted and peacefully prayed with others outside an abortion clinic. When a couple approached the clinic, someone asked if one of the prayer warriors could pray for the couple in Spanish. Deanna speaks a little Spanish, just enough to give her testimony. They listened and thanked her but entered the clinic anyway. Moments later, they came back out and gave her a thumbs-up—they had decided to keep their baby. "I believe a lot of people have devalued motherhood," she says. "Confessing our worst stuff literally brings life to people."[1]

Deanna's Lessons from the Ditch

- *Learn to direct your thoughts.* I knew in my heart that I
  wanted to be a mother, but I allowed my thoughts to be
  manipulated by the media, pop culture, and other
  people. Get your truth from the Word of God and
  through your own prayer and connection with Christ.
- *Aspire first to be at peace when you make decisions.* If you
  are not at peace, you may create your own setback—and
  it may be a devastating one that cannot be undone.
- *When you cause your own setback, accept God's forgiveness.*
  And forgive yourself. "All have sinned and fall short of
  the glory of God" (Romans 3:23).
- *As you pursue your dreams, stay grounded.* When you get
  knocked off your path, this grounding will lead you
  onto your authentic path.

FOUR

What Are You Most Afraid Of?

Calling Out Your Fears
Is the First Step to Conquering Them

Afanter life takes an unexpected twist and you find yourself reeling, grabbing for something stable to hold on to, God's voice isn't the only one vying for your attention. The enemy is hard at work, whispering seeds of doubt and outright lies to get you to give up or become distracted.

John 10:10 spells out the enemy's mission statement: "The thief comes only to steal and kill and destroy." The easiest time for him to accomplish his purpose is when you're already down, when you're disoriented and afraid.

I remember vividly the doubts and painful lies the enemy whispered in my ear when my first marriage ended:

- *Drag your fears into the light.*

- *Don't catastrophize.*

- *Arm yourself with faith and truth.*

"Your life is over."

"You won't be able to bounce back from this."

"It's too late. You'll never have children."

"Churches won't invite you to speak anymore. You're divorced."

"You don't have a right to write books and give advice anymore."

"Six years of your life have been stolen and you'll never get them back."

I had to start talking back to those lies rather than buying into them. True, my life wasn't going to turn out the way I planned it. But God still had a good plan for my life. When I made the choice to believe that, I could counter the enemy's lies by declaring the truth:

"You have a lot of life ahead. It just looks different from what you thought it would. Be grateful for your life. Make the most of it."

"Of course you'll bounce back. Maybe you don't feel like it right this minute, but you will. Resilience is in your blood!"

"It's not too late. Believe God for children—whether biological or not. And if you don't get to have children, then God must have another plan for you. Embrace His will, whatever it is. Trust Him and choose joy."

"Sure, maybe some churches won't invite you to speak. But many more will invite you. And your compassion for others' pain will grow because of your experience and make your message stronger than ever."

"Of course you have the right to write! It is your divinely inspired mission. The enemy would just love for you to stop living your purpose! Don't give him that satisfaction."

"Nothing in my life is in vain. I will make sure God gets the glory."

During our weak moments, fighting the enemy is undeniably hard. But we do not fight alone.

A Power Greater Than Fear

You may know the scripture, "For God has not given us a spirit of fear, but of power and of love and of a sound mind" (2 Timothy 1:7, NKJV). It is important to note that this scripture does not say that we won't feel fear or that it is wrong to feel fear. It says that God has not given us a spirit of fear. That means we are not to be bound up in fear. We are not to allow fear to dictate our actions or to paralyze us.

God knows we will feel fear because He repeatedly gives us scriptures instructing His people to be courageous:

> Be strong and courageous. Do not be afraid or terrified because of them, for the LORD your God goes with you; he will never leave you nor forsake you. (Deuteronomy 31:6)

> Be strong and courageous, because you will lead these people to inherit the land I swore to their ancestors to give them. Be strong and very courageous. (Joshua 1:6–7)

> Have I not commanded you? Be strong and courageous. Do not be afraid; do not be discouraged, for the LORD your God will be with you wherever you go. (Joshua 1:9)

> Act with courage, and may the LORD be with those who do well. (2 Chronicles 19:11)

> Be strong and courageous. Do not be afraid or discouraged because of the king of Assyria and the vast army with him, for there is a greater power with us than with him. (2 Chronicles 32:7)

Take courage! It is I. Don't be afraid. (Matthew 14:27)

Be on your guard; stand firm in the faith; be courageous; be strong. Do everything in love. (1 Corinthians 16:13–14)

God knows we will feel fear, which is why He reminds us so often to take courage—to believe that He is with us and that He is more powerful than any enemy we may face.

Fear is the enemy's weapon of choice to get you out of the will of God, to keep you from reaching your destiny. But the enemy does not get to choose whether or not you will bow to fear. The decision is yours. You can determine right now that you will face your challenges with courage. You will not entertain doubt. You will operate in faith, not fear.

That is exactly what Jacqueline Jakes chose to do when a seizure changed the course of her life in 1982. One moment, she was a healthy twenty-nine-year-old mother starting her day at work; the next moment, she was having a seizure, which led to brain surgery. "I spent the next ten years trying to regain my emotional and physical health," she explains.

She described for me her long road to recovery. "The worst part, I think, was being under attack," says Jacqueline, author of *God's Trophy Women* and *Sister Wit.* "It was what I felt mentally and physically—the anxiety and depression. The anxiety was a level 10."

Anxiety is a form of fear. It is a fear of what might be coming, just around the corner, and the fear that you won't be able to handle it.

"People knew I had undergone brain surgery, but on the outside I looked fine," she says. "Inwardly, there were unimaginable attacks… It was like my soul and my spirit had split. I was in this place where I recognized and knew everyone, but I was trying to find the old me. I was not the person I had been before the surgery. I was groping around trying to find myself, trying to get back to normalcy.

"I don't think people understand what a blessing it is to just feel normal," she continues. "It was terrifying to be in an altered state. I knew I was not who I had been before. I don't remember how long that period lasted, but it was a dark, dark place."

How did she get through this dark period? "Faith and courage," she says. "I have always been a believer in the Lord Jesus Christ. Since I was a child, I always believed in God. I pressed in to God. I couldn't make others understand how horrific and terrible this is. I picked up my Bible and sat on this sofa in my horrible little house. I went from Genesis to Revelation. I said, 'Your Word says you're a healer. I am believing You will heal me.'"

Jacqueline says there was no room for doubt at that point in her life. "Like a starving dog after a bone, I couldn't give up," she says. "I had a child to raise. I didn't have time to doubt."[1]

There are moments in your life when you can't spare the time or energy to doubt. All of your strength needs to be poured into your recovery. Your energy must be focused on believing rather than doubting, and on faith rather than on fear.

I don't know where you are right now. I don't know how deep your ditch is, but I do know that ditches are dark and lonely. Now is the time to muster faith like you never have before and refuse to back down. That is the essence of courage: to stare fear in the face and keep pushing forward. And you can do so in the confidence that God is present with you.

CALL YOUR FEARS BY NAME

The most debilitating fears often hide just below the surface of our lives. They hover at the edges of our conversations as we skirt the real issues in our lives, not wanting to appear vulnerable or anxious. Or perhaps we suspect that acknowledging our deepest fears will somehow make them come true.

We keep our deepest fears in the dark where we can't see them, yet that's exactly where the enemy wants them! If they remain there, you will never get a chance to see that while they may be scary, *you can handle them.* Left in the dark, they grow into an unconquerable monster that has the power to destroy you. Brought into the light, they can be addressed, analyzed, and overcome.

Remember how Dorothy and her friends were terrified of the Wizard of Oz? No one had actually seen the wizard, and with his booming voice and special effects, no one dared to say something that might arouse the wrath of the great and powerful Oz. But when Dorothy finally mustered the courage to make some demands of the wizard, it turned out he was just an unimpressive imposter, hiding behind a facade of machinery and gadgets. Similarly, our fears often appear more frightful and powerful than they actually are.

Rather than trying to pretend away our fears, the best way to deal with them is to systematically call them out: name them for what they are, and confront them directly, in the light of truth.

Consider the vivid doubts and fears the enemy taunted me with after my marriage ended. For almost a year, I was deeply pained by the thought that I might never experience motherhood. I love children and have long looked forward to the day when I would have some of my own. I hadn't previously felt anxious about my biological clock ticking, but the idea of starting over in my late thirties made me seriously consider the possibility that maybe my dream of bearing children would not come true. This fear sat heavily on my shoulders until one day, as I sat in bed praying, pondering, and meditating, I boldly looked it in the face.

What if I don't ever have a child? I asked myself. It was a question I had not wanted to answer because the idea brought such grief—not only because of the possible loss of motherhood but also because of years lost, seemingly wasted.

I am generally not a regretful person, and I don't believe regret is a place where God wants us to remain. So I asked a more empowering question, the same one I asked you to answer in the last chapter: *How did I end up here?* I examined the decisions I'd made that contributed to my circumstances. It wasn't about pointing fingers, but about owning my role and learning from my pain. I find that when I admit and learn from my mistakes, I am less likely to repeat them.

As I sat there, it occurred to me that I did not want to continue operating in fear about motherhood. It felt like bondage.

So I asked the question again, because it was the question that forced me to face my fear: *What if you don't ever have children?* I didn't just ponder the question in my head; I felt it in my heart as I visualized my life ten, twenty, even fifty years into the future. Then I thought of all the happy women I've known or admired who are not mothers. I considered the children already in my life whom I have the opportunity to influence. I imagined the opportunities I might pursue if I didn't take on the responsibilities of parenting.

And I thought about God's will for my life.

Ah. Now I was getting somewhere. His perfect will was what I wanted—and what I still want. I suddenly felt a burden lift. *It is what it is, Valorie,* were the words in my spirit. *You have a good life. You have time. With God, all things are possible. If you let go of the need to understand how those things will be possible, you will be free of the burden of fear and uncertainty.*

I had faced my fear—and it didn't look all that scary. If I didn't have children, then I would trust that was God's will for my life, and if it was God's will, life would be just fine. As I embraced what is—rather than dwelling on what if—my faith in what might be became stronger. Accepting that I might not get what I wanted allowed me to believe in my dream without holding it so tightly that I crushed it.

Now it's your turn to be bold and courageous. Start by calling out your fears. Face them. Bring them into the light. Ask, What if that fear comes true? With God's love and grace, how will I handle it?

Take a moment and be honest with yourself: what are the deep fears that linger beneath the surface of your life?

For each fear you listed, answer this question: what will happen if this fear becomes reality?

Look back at the list above. Which of your fears, if realized, would pose a serious challenge that would require a great deal of effort to conquer? By contrast, which of your fears are either unfounded or, if they came true, would be manageable?

For each fear that would pose a major challenge if it became reality, what can you do to prevent or cope with it? What specific actions will you need to take to muster the courage?

For each fear that remains a genuine possibility and would pose a serious problem, what scripture(s) will encourage you and help you stay focused if you must deal with the issue?

If God were whispering guidance and advice in your ear right now, what would He tell you about the fears that grip you most?

STOP CATASTROPHIZING

We've seen how minimizing the impact of a crisis is a form of denial that can keep you from bouncing back quickly and completely. But blowing a crisis out of proportion—another manifestation of fear—can also keep you stuck. Psychologists call it "catastrophizing." It's what happens when your negative thoughts about a situation spiral out of control.

It can happen with even the simplest of situations: Your sister is five minutes late meeting you for lunch. You call her cell phone but don't get an answer. Immediately, you start catastrophizing. You imagine she's been in a terrible car accident. She was probably rushing because the last time she was late you were annoyed and criticized her for not being more considerate of others' time. You just know that since she rushed out the door to meet you, she left her purse behind, which is why she doesn't have her cell phone. Because she has no purse, she has no identification. She's been rushed to the hospital, but she is in such bad condition that she couldn't give them her name. You and your family will have to call every hospital looking for her. She might die alone—and it will be all your fault because you couldn't show a little mercy for your sister's habitual tardiness!

This scenario might seem far-fetched. But truth be told, many of us catastrophize on a regular basis. We can go from thinking *My sister's late* to *My sister's dead and unidentified in a hospital* in about ten seconds. That's how quickly our thoughts can spiral out of control. If you don't catastrophize, you probably know someone who does. And even if it's not the norm for you, such thinking is often triggered by setbacks, major life changes, or any stress-inducing situation.

Resilient People Know...

Faith conquers fear. Expect to feel fear when you face major challenges, then move forward despite it, believing you have the strength to make it through to the other side.

When much of what you have known to be true about your life suddenly changes, the natural result is a sense of uncertainty...doubt...fear. Fear is at the root of catastrophizing, which can blossom into anxiety—sometimes paralyzing anxiety and anguish. In fact, a catastrophizer will imagine the worst and convince himself that the ditch is just the beginning of the trouble, that there is no way out, and that the domino effect of tragedies will never end.

Have you found yourself pondering the worst-case, irrational scenarios resulting from your setback? Answer the following questions:

When you think about your situation, what thoughts spiral out of control and create paralyzing anxiety?

When do you tend to have these thoughts?

How do you feel when you entertain these thoughts?

In light of your circumstances, what would be a more empowering thought for you to have?

What feeling would that thought create for you?

TAKING EVERY THOUGHT CAPTIVE

The chart below identifies the core thoughts behind some of these common negative emotions and what actions you can take to move beyond them.

Emotion	Core Thought	Action
Embarrassment	Others will not accept me.	Accept where you are, let go of others' expectations, and give yourself permission to move forward.
Disappointment	My expectations were not met.	Mourn your loss, if needed. Then adjust expectations or find a healthy way to get them met.
Anger	My rights were violated. A boundary was crossed.	Choose forgiveness. Refuse to be bitter. Let go so you can be free.
Resentment	Someone or something caused intentional harm without remorse.	Forgive. When appropriate, express your feelings.
Uncertainty	The future feels beyond my control.	Get comfortable with not knowing. Have faith that God knows, and trust that He cares.

Emotion	Core Thought	Action
Guilt	I did something wrong and caused harm.	Ask forgiveness. Compensate for harm caused, if possible. And forgive yourself.
Sadness	I lost something meaningful to me.	Mourn your loss. Then find something for which to be grateful. Choose to move forward.
Despair	I feel no sense of hope for my future.	Renew your hope by strengthening your relationship with God. Consider counseling with a therapist or pastor.
Shame	Beyond *doing* something wrong, I *am* something wrong. I have something unacceptable to hide.	Forgive yourself. Recognize that you are acceptable in God's eyes. Make a list of your positive character traits. If necessary, ask a friend to help.
Anxiety	I am afraid about the future.	Put things into perspective. Focus on the present moment. Pray.
Fear	I am more focused on what may go wrong than on what may go right.	Choose courage and boldness. Remember, the Lord is with you wherever you go.

CONQUER NEGATIVE THINKING

Fear is not only at the root of anxiety but also feeds many other negative emotions that can accompany a setback or unexpected turn in life: embarrassment, disappointment, anger, resentment, uncertainty, guilt, despair, sadness, and shame. These emotions, too, need to be acknowledged and dealt with. Some will naturally run their course. Others need to be worked through intentionally.

The Bible gives a lot of sound advice when it comes to taking charge of our thoughts and emotions. One of the most powerful yet underused verses is 2 Corinthians 10:5: "We demolish arguments and every pretension that sets itself up against the knowledge of God, and we take captive every thought to make it obedient to Christ." The King James Version says, "Casting down imaginations, and every high thing that exalteth itself against the knowledge of God, and bringing into captivity every thought to the obedience of Christ."

Whether you call them "arguments" or "imaginations," one of the most significant steps you can take right now is to demolish irrational, negative thinking. So let's talk about how to take every thought captive.

First, it's important to realize that we don't necessarily control the thoughts that come into our minds. In fact, you may have been thinking positively today when someone's unexpected comment threw you off track and sent your thoughts scurrying down paths of worry and anxiety.

However, while we can't necessarily control what crosses our minds, *we do control what we choose to dwell on.* Think of it like your front door. Anyone can knock on it, but you decide whether or not to invite the visitor in.

What counterproductive thoughts have you been inviting in? Here are a few of the particularly destructive thoughts that can hinder your ability to recover from a setback:

- *You'll never work your way out of here. You shouldn't even bother to try.*
- *Your life is over. Your best days are behind you.*
- *You'll never recover from this.*
- *You should be ashamed. You don't have the right to recover from such an embarrassing setback.*
- *God is punishing you.*
- *It's too late to get back on track. You'll never get your lost years/money/time back.*
- *You don't have what it takes to bounce back.*

The thoughts can be debilitating, especially if you don't call them out. The first step toward taking thoughts captive is acknowledging they exist in the first place.

What negative thoughts are undermining your recovery? Make a list here:

Now, when these thoughts knock at the doorstep of your mind, remember that you've already identified them as unwelcome, so don't invite them in! Take them captive by locking them out. There are a few ways you can do that.

1. Create a Gate to the Neighborhood

One of the best ways to keep out counterproductive thoughts is to limit their access to you—make it harder for them to even get to your door. So try creating a barrier—decide to move your mind to a gated neighborhood, so to speak. You can do this by noticing the activities, people, and circumstances that seem to usher these thoughts in. Is there a particularly negative person in your life who catastrophizes for you? Do certain television shows or media put you in a frame of mind to feel sorry for yourself? Does a particular activity always lead you to see your situation as worse than it is? If you answered yes to any of these, make a list of ways you can limit your exposure to these triggers.

2. Dispute It, Then Tell It to Leave

When a thought comes knocking, don't make it easy for that thought to come in and hang out in your mind. If the thought is untrue, say so—out loud. Talk back to your counterproductive thoughts. Say, "That's not true because..." or "Actually, a better way of looking at this is..." In doing so, you are calling out the lie and telling the truth. You are, in essence, telling it to go away. If some element of truth is wrapped in the negative thought that comes knocking, you can acknowledge it—and then acknowledge God's ability to help you deal with it. For example, "Yes, life will never be the same, but I have the strength to handle the change and the faith to believe that on the other side of this, better days lie ahead." Accept the truth, but send the counterproductive negativity packing.

3. Ignore It

Some thoughts aren't even worth acknowledging. They are so irrational and futile that you don't even need to waste precious energy disputing them. Have you ever had a stranger come to the door when you didn't have time to talk? You just pretended you weren't home and went about your business, right? Eventually, the person left. Proverbs 26:20 says, "Without wood a fire goes out; without a gossip a quarrel dies down." When it comes to negative thoughts, the same principle applies. Don't add wood to a potential fire. Let some negative thoughts die out by refusing to give your energy to them.

4. Replace the Thought

Replace counterproductive thoughts, such as the ones you listed earlier, with productive thoughts. Joshua 1:8 says, "Keep this Book of the Law always on your lips; meditate on it day and night, so that you may be careful to do everything written in it. Then you will be prosperous and successful." Meditating on the Word of God puts you in the right frame of mind to push through your challenge. It will give you strength, wisdom, and the perseverance you need right now.

As you learn to face your fears and negative emotions, recognize that they are weapons of the enemy. You must first bring them into the light so you can see what you are fighting. Be curious about your fears. Ask the hard questions and answer them honestly.

Be bold.

Be courageous.

Have faith.

Trust God.

You Have Everything You Need

Use the Power of Your *Thoughts*

Your thoughts are the most important asset you control. Do not allow the enemy a foothold by entertaining negative, anxiety-producing thoughts about your future. Focus your thoughts on being bold and courageous.

Use the Power of Your *Words*

When fears throw a punch, fight back! Speak to your fears. Put them in their place. Use the Word of God, use the truth, and use your past successes to combat negative, unhealthy thoughts.

Use the Power of Your *Actions*

Take a look at the anxious and fearful thoughts you wrote down in this chapter. Identify an act of courage—whether it's having an honest conversation with someone or making a change in your routine—that will help you loosen the grip fear has on your thought life.

Use the Power of *Relationships*

Talk to a trusted friend about one of your biggest fears, and discuss whether or not it's a realistic concern. Use the questions in this chapter as a guide for your conversation.

Use the Power of *Prayer*

Lord, I am dealing with fears and emotions that threaten to keep me in the ditch if I don't conquer them. Strengthen me with a level of boldness and courage I've never had before. Help me remember You are with me wherever I go. Give me a greater measure of faith to break free of strongholds and fears so I can dig out of my ditch and find my path. Amen.

Triumph Over Trials: Lillian's Story

Lillian Sparks and her husband, Rev. Steve Sparks, both twenty-two years old, were just two months into their first position in ministry when their first child was born. Doctors had not detected any issues prior to the birth, so Lillian expected a healthy baby. "We didn't know we were genetic carriers of an incurable skin disease," Lillian explains. "Bryon lost 80 percent of his skin upon birth." Baby Bryon shouldn't have lived, but he was a fighter. Even so, the experience was utterly devastating.

"I was numb," Lillian says. "I had a hard time believing this could happen to me. I remember the day they took him from the regular nursery to another part of the hospital to pediatric intensive care. They wheeled him to my room. We couldn't touch him. He was covered with blisters that hung like balloons all over his body. Every time he would kick, more skin would come off and stick to the sheets as he cried."

Overwhelmed and stunned, Lillian and her husband called on their faith. "My husband asked me, 'Do you remember the prayer I prayed when we were engaged? I prayed about our future. I told God we don't care what it takes. We want our anointing to be different. God is answering that prayer.'" So in an act of faith, Lillian and Steve prayed together for Bryon, and they prayed for their own strength to deal with the monumental challenge before them.

"I believe that what the enemy meant for evil, God meant for good," Lillian says. "The day we prayed over that incubator, it became our altar. We said, 'We accept this as his parents, as part of Your will for our lives.'" It was no easy feat, but they persevered and did just that—and had three more children after Bryon, all of them healthy.

Over the next twenty-one years, Bryon would need 24/7 personal care. "I changed bandages for one and a half hours every morning and one and a half to two hours every night," Lillian recalls. Bryon endured twenty different operations over the years, many just to keep him alive. His condition was so rare that some of his procedures took place in other countries, where specialists agreed to help him, including a three-month stay in Italy, three months in Spain, and six months in Germany. During these medical treatments, Bryon was away from his family. Some of these treatments were therapeutic, improving his condition and reducing his pain. The challenges persisted, yet Bryon persisted as well. In fact, his nickname—given by his pediatric surgeon—was "Tough Cookie." It became the title of Lillian's first book about Bryon's struggles.[2]

He did many things that were not expected of someone with his disabilities. "He had a beautiful singing voice. He had a voice like an angel," Lillian recalls. He was invited multiple times to perform for the Brooklyn Tabernacle with its world-famous choir. As a teenager, he taught children's Sunday school and learned to drive. "He was the safest driver in the family," Lillian recalls with a chuckle. And he finished school and went on to college.

Bryon never weighed more than fifty pounds because he never got his second growth genes. Eventually the challenges of his condition became more than his body was able to bear. He was diagnosed with skin cancer, likely due to his many surgeries and scarring. He had a cancerous tumor in his hand, which became four times larger than normal. During the last seven months of his life, the cancer spread to his lungs. He had back pain. His weight dropped to a mere twenty-eight pounds.

Lillian points out that she got through her son's illness because of the attitude she chose. Often, people who face a setback such as a loved one's death or their own personal challenge want to place blame—whether on God or someone else, Lillian says. "But that doesn't bring the person back, and it doesn't change what you are walking through at that moment.

"Life is filled with choices," she continues. "A long time ago as a young mother with Bryon, I *chose* to have joy. Bryon also modeled that. He never complained about the pain. He always had something positive to say. Even on his death bed, he was thinking of others. He wrote a prophetic letter to each of his three siblings of what he saw for their lives. It was October, and he gave everyone a Christmas gift because he knew he wouldn't be here. He planned his funeral, with his friends and cousins as his pallbearers. He asked his aunt Faith to sing 'Great Is Thy Faithfulness' at the funeral. He told me, 'It's okay, Mom. I get a new body. Either way, living or dying, I cannot lose!'"

When Bryon was about to have his arm amputated up to his elbow, he asked his parents, "What am I going to do when they take off my arm?" Lillian says her husband told him, "Bryon, you are going to do what you've done for twenty-one years. You are going to dig deep and find the courage that only God can give you." It was Commitment #3 at work: I will dig deep to unearth all the courage I need. Of the Five Commitments, Lillian says this is the one they all called on most.

The next day, Bryon was in the hospital and on the phone with his grandmother, who began crying. Lillian overheard him comforting her. "Nanny, don't cry for me," he said. "God isn't done using my life. You know, I started to feel sorry for myself the other day, and God told me, *'You still have a voice. You can sing. You can still hug people and love the kids in your Sunday school class. You can run with the legs you have.'* I have so much to be grateful for. Don't you dare cry for me, Nanny."

That resilient spirit led Bryon to learn to feed himself again. He found a way to connect a spoon to the end of his amputated arm and eat. And he taught himself to write with his other hand.

Several months after that conversation between Bryon and Nanny, Lillian lost her son. Bryon was twenty-one. She says many of her victories in persevering through her child's severe disability happened through worship. "Sometimes you stop reading the Word or going to church because you don't feel like it. But you have to keep serving and loving God no matter what." She says she had breakthroughs because she was in the right place at the right time and the Spirit of God showed up. Sometimes, it happened while playing the piano in church or reading a scripture. She kept serving and God kept showing up.[3]

LILLIAN'S LESSONS FROM THE DITCH

- *Keep loving and worshiping God.* No matter how difficult things get, do not give up on God. He is with you. He is your source of strength. Let Him grow you through your trials.

- *Keep living!* Don't stop living your life because of your setback. Celebrate life. Have your Christmas holidays. Enjoy your family. Somewhere along the way, God will heal your heart. You will have your breakthrough. It is a conscious choice you must make, and it cannot be based on your feelings because sometimes you don't feel like living life to the fullest. But that is what Jesus came for, that we might have life to the fullest, until it overflows (John 10:10).

- *Hang on to your marriage.* Parents of children with disabilities often end up getting divorced. Lillian says it is hard when the child's needs take priority over the relationship. You might be about to spend time with each other, and suddenly that child is crying in pain. The child needs you. So you have to work that much harder to make time for each other. Take care of your marriage. Refuse to allow a double tragedy—the death or disability of your child and a divorce. You cannot be in the marriage just for what you can get out of it. It is not always easy, but stick with it.

FIVE

How Can You Regain Your Confidence?

*Finding Stability and Strength
to Prepare for Your Comeback*

- *Let go of what you
  cannot change.*

- *Believe that your
  choices will make a
  difference.*

- *Tap into your
  strengths and
  conserve your
  energy.*

We've talked about the disorienting effects of an unexpected setback and the need to give yourself time to stabilize before you move forward. So just what does it mean to get stable? It means knowing where you are and having what you need in place so you can move forward. It requires you to believe that you have the ability to get out of the ditch—that you can handle what life has thrown your way and that you will thrive even though things are not going the way you planned.

Marie was in her early fifties when her husband died suddenly of a heart attack at work. Since college, John had been Marie's constant companion and the love of her life, and she'd thought they would have many years ahead of them. They had planned to move to the South after retirement, then pursue their dream of traveling along the East Coast in their sailboat. Nothing had prepared her for this unwelcome change in the future she'd envisioned.

Six years after his death, Marie had still not fully processed her loss. Their two adult children worried that she would never accept her new reality. In fact, their mother told them she coped with their father's death by telling herself he was away on a long trip. She refused to give away his clothes, and she kept many of his personal possessions in the house. Any time one of the kids tried to suggest it might be time to make some changes, she resisted. She told them they just didn't understand. They realized that as long as she remained in denial she would be unable to move forward and embrace a new season in her life. Secretly, she realized it too. But she was too afraid to look ahead into an unknown future.

Bernard's setback was much different, and yet, he was just as resistant to accepting reality as Marie. For twelve years his construction business had thrived, but projects had dwindled drastically in recent years. Bernard and his wife, Candace, felt increasingly stressed as their financial situation spiraled out of control. They needed to downsize their lifestyle, but Bernard clung to the possibility of a sudden turnaround. He fought to hold on to the business, but debts and dried-up revenue eventually forced him to take a job offer from a friend and a 40 percent pay cut.

For Bernard, a proud, hard-working man who had dreamed of owning a business his entire life, closing up his company left him feeling defeated and embarrassed. All sorts of negative thoughts plagued him daily: Didn't he have what it took to succeed? Why didn't he prepare better for the storm?

During the height of his business success, he and his wife had purchased a five-bedroom home in a nice suburb of Tampa. For years when he pulled into the driveway each night after work, he'd savored the sight of this ultimate symbol of his success. *Dad would be so proud,* he often thought. Now he could no longer afford the dream. Candace convinced him to put the house on the market, and after ten months, they finally got a decent offer. Candace felt relieved at the thought of getting out from under the financial burden of the house. She loved their home, but she knew their family didn't need a fancy place to be happy together—they could rent a modest home about ten miles away in a more affordable sub-urb. Bernard, on the other hand, struggled terribly with the idea of moving. He couldn't forgive himself for "failing," as he saw it. He regularly rehashed everything that had happened in the business, wondering why things had gone wrong. He hesitated to accept the offer on the house, still looking for some way to hang on to his dream.

LETTING GO OF WHAT WAS, ACCEPTING WHAT IS

If you can look at your adversity in a way that fosters resilience, stability will come more easily. You will feel less stressed, and as a result, your transition will likely take less out of you. You can climb your way out of the ditch in a calm, steadfast manner, or you can waste precious energy by kicking and screaming your way out. Yes, either way you'll make it out, but climbing out calmly is a lot less stressful.

I'd imagine that at some point you've heard what's commonly known as the Serenity Prayer:

> *God, grant me the serenity*
> *To accept the things I cannot change,*
> *Courage to change the things I can,*
> *And wisdom to know the difference.*[1]

Such a simple prayer. But now, as you navigate unexpected changes in your life, it can hold new meaning. In the midst of upheaval, our most powerful longing is for serenity, a sense of peace amid the chaos in our lives.

Peace is hard to come by when life feels so out of control, when we see ourselves at the mercy of forces outside ourselves. The truth is, even in the calm and normal seasons of life, we don't have as much control as we'd like to think. Certainly, as we've seen, our choices have an impact on the direction our lives will take. And the wiser our choices, the better our chances of staying on track. But no one makes wise choices 100 percent of the time. And unexpected things will happen despite our best efforts and intentions.

When events don't unfold just as you would like, the smartest, least stressful approach you can take is to accept that it is what it is. You may wish it were different. Perhaps it should be different. But it isn't. When you accept the reality of a situation rather than ruminating over what *should be,* you empower yourself to come up with solutions that will help you move forward. No longer stuck in the past, you are free to focus your energy on improving the situation for the future. You don't blame anyone. You simply accept the things you cannot change and go about changing the things you can. Of course, you may need to grieve what has been lost before you can focus on rebuilding—but don't let yourself get stuck in grief mode.

Declaring aloud, "It is what it is!" releases you from the need to analyze, manipulate, or change a situation in order to have peace. It acknowledges that life isn't perfect—and that it doesn't need to be for you to have peace and joy. Your satisfaction doesn't depend on what happens; it's rooted in the certainty that "all things work together for good to those who love God, to those who are the called according to His purpose"

(Romans 8:28, NKJV). You may not be able to see that purpose at the moment, but you refuse to view yourself as a victim of either the whims of circumstance or the actions of another person; instead you declare that where you are now is part of your God-designed destiny.

In your particular situation, is it time to accept a reality that you've tried to deny? What would it look like to let go? What shift will you have to make to move forward in a positive way?

Bottom line: It's time to accept what you cannot change. It may be devastating, frustrating, or upsetting. But resisting the inevitable is a waste of your much-needed energy. The sooner you accept what is, the sooner you can get out of the ditch.

Remember the words of the apostle Paul as he sat in a filthy jail cell after his life was thrown off course:

> I have learned to be content whatever the circumstances. I know what it is to be in need, and I know what it is to have plenty. I have learned the secret of being content in any and every situation, whether well fed or hungry, whether living in plenty or in want. I can do all this through him who gives me strength. (Philippians 4:11–13)

In the midst of a major challenge, "being content" doesn't mean being happy about what's happening. Instead, it means trusting God to walk with you through it. It means not feeling sorry for yourself. It means accepting that sometimes life isn't fair, but you can choose to rise to the occasion—to find the strength of character to persevere anyway. It means knowing with all your heart that you can do all things through Him who gives you strength. It means not worrying about the future, and choosing to think positively. Remember Paul's words to the Philippians:

> Do not be anxious about anything, but in every situation, by prayer and petition, with thanksgiving, present your requests to God. And the peace of God, which transcends all understanding, will guard your hearts and your minds in Christ Jesus. Finally, brothers and sisters, whatever is true, whatever is noble, whatever is right, whatever is pure, whatever is lovely, whatever is admirable—if anything is excellent or praiseworthy—think about such things. (4:6–8)

Take a deep breath and remind yourself of all that you have to be grateful for. You can choose peace in any moment. Doing so is not always easy, but it is always possible.

COURAGE TO CHANGE THE THINGS YOU CAN

Of course, accepting that "it is what it is" does not mean passively lying back and giving up. While we can't control everything that happens to us, we are in complete control of how we choose to respond.

Right now, your confidence may be a bit bruised. Things you thought you knew for sure are suddenly in question. Setbacks can sometimes cause us to doubt who we are and what we are capable of. While that is a common reaction, you won't find stability in that place of doubt. James 1:6–8 says, "The one who doubts is like a wave of the sea, blown and tossed by the wind. That person should not expect to receive anything from the Lord. Such a person is double-minded and unstable in all they do."

There is a phenomenon known as *learned helplessness,* a state in which you come to believe nothing you do matters. When you face disappointments, remember that the enemy wants you to believe things will not get better—that this is the beginning of the end. Your job right now is to believe that the situation can be turned around, or if not, that with God's help you have what it takes to forge ahead and pursue a new course. You may be traveling with a limp, but nonetheless you'll be moving forward.

This simple, yet powerful, belief that you can move forward is known as *self-efficacy,* which simply means that you believe you can accomplish what you set out to do. By doing a little bit at a time, you build self-efficacy. It isn't about taking one giant step, but a series of small ones that build on each other.

Resilient People Know. . .

Achieving small goals builds self-efficacy—
your belief in your abilities. So identify a
small, achievable goal you will pursue today to
further your comeback.

Dr. Suzanne Kobasa, a psychologist and researcher at the City University of New York, has identified three commonalities that distinguish those who show resilience in the face of stress and challenges.[2] Those three factors are *control, commitment,* and *challenge.* Let's look at each of these factors to see how you can tap into them to increase your sense of stability and build your confidence so that you are ready to move forward once more.

Control

Control refers to a belief in your ability to influence the outcome of your circumstances. A person who feels she has *no* control of what happens when faced with a challenge will feel more stressed than someone in the same situation who feels she has *some* degree of control. The ability to exert control is not enough; you must *believe you have that ability.* It is the belief that impacts your stress level. Those who don't view themselves as helpless, vulnerable victims believe they can take back the reins. They are moved to action to influence what happens next in their lives. As a result, they are often quite successful despite challenges and setbacks.

As we've seen, it's pointless to try to control everything. A more effective approach is to get clear about the outcome you want to see unfold. Then ask yourself, *What steps can I take to create that outcome?* You have to believe that what you do matters. Your attitude matters. Your choices matter. Refuse to get distracted by the drama or frustrations of your challenge; instead, remain grounded and calm by focusing on the things you can do something about.

Commitment

Those who demonstrate resilience despite multiple stressors and challenges in their lives tend to be highly engaged in the work they do. Whatever work they do day to day, inside the home or out, they are committed to it. Their commitment—whether to something or someone—gives them a deep sense of purpose and meaning, a reason to move forward.

Part of stabilizing yourself to move forward is finding your motivation. Your motivation is your "why." It's the reason you decide that you *will* push through this challenge and you *will* triumph, no matter what. For Jacqueline Jakes, trying to recover after her brain injury, her motivation was taking care of her daughter. For me, I found inspiration in what God spoke to me during my quietest moments: that my best days were ahead of me if I would just trust Him. I committed myself to believing Him and hanging on to those words.

What are the values—the priorities—that inspire you and give you a sense of purpose? Tapping into these will fuel your perseverance for the days ahead.

Challenge

Those who demonstrate less stress and more resilience in the midst of adversity tend to view change not as a reason for stress, but as a chance to stretch and grow.

Research shows that some of the most resilient people are those who have dealt with multiple stressors throughout their lives. Rather than letting those challenges defeat them, they've seen them as opportunities to grow. In her book *God's Trophy Women,* Jacqueline Jakes calls it "the secret of the strong."[3]

"When your life is layered with conflict and challenge," she told me, "I think you are stronger than the average person. I was not liked as a child. The girls in the neighborhood always wanted to fight me. It helped build my relationship with God. It helped me deal with trouble because He was preparing me for the fight of my life. I'd come up in a hostile environment. I'd been through a separation and divorce, was a single mom, and had buried my father."[4] By age twenty-nine, when she had the brain surgery that would take her ten years to recover from, she was strong enough to deal with the challenge.

A great measure of faith is needed to believe that something good can result from life's disappointments and defeats—that you can emerge from adversity better and stronger than before. It is like living in two worlds: your current reality and your future potential. And the two can look so devastatingly different that at times you'll ask, *Am I just kidding myself?* This is the time to remember what faith is: the substance of things *hoped for* and the evidence of things *not seen* (Hebrews 11:1, NKJV). This is what makes you different as a believer. Believers *believe* in a God who is at work behind the scenes. You believe the impossible is possible. You don't make your decisions based purely on what you see but on the Word of God and God's ability to speak directly to you through the Holy Spirit. You are not a doubter. You are a believer.

Adversity will show you who you really are. I believe you have more strength than you realize. If you approach unexpected life changes in the right way, you can do more than just survive. On the other side, you can be even better off than you were before this difficulty intruded into your life. I understand that right now such a possibility might seem more than a little unlikely, but this stage of your life brings an opportunity for your faith to stretch and grow in ways it otherwise never could.

What frustrates you most about your setback?

What aspect of this frustration do you have control over?

What aspect of this frustration do you have absolutely no control over?

What step will you take to accept the thing you cannot change—in other words, the thing you have no control over?

Start from Your Strengths

I find it particularly encouraging that we don't get our strengths after our setbacks—we already have them. Before you were formed in your mother's womb, God knew you, and He equipped you to handle everything that would come your way!

Remember Kevin Wolitzky, my high school classmate, whose baseball accident permanently paralyzed him? The hope, optimism, and discipline that propel him now can be traced back to long before his accident when, as a teenager, he ranked twentieth in the state for cross-country, was named all-state in three sports, and won a full scholarship to play baseball in college. Those strengths were at the core of his training; they fueled his perseverance through grueling workouts and a rigorous competition schedule. Commenting on the connection between his athletic background and his ability to be resilient in the face of paralysis, he says, "All of that discipline helped me to never give up. It helped me to cope." And when he is asked what gave him the confidence, as a quadriplegic, to ask girls out on dates, he says, "I didn't let it stop me from asking girls out. I never really quit. I always believed it would work out."

You can often discover your strengths by simply noticing what you say about your circumstances. Just listening to Kevin talk about his life, you realize that optimism is part of his DNA. He believed he could still accomplish many things that others would assume were no longer options for him. Because he believed, he took action based on those beliefs. Those actions led to such accomplishments as a career as an engineer, a marriage to a loving woman, and three healthy, beautiful children.

You were born with innate strengths that are unique to you. Your strengths empower you to engage with the world around you, effectively relate to the people who cross your path, and make a difference in a way that only you can. Though previously you may not have explicitly identified your strengths, you've called on them time and again to get you through tough spots or to help you excel in work and life. Now you simply need to tap into them more deliberately as you prepare to climb onto the path of the life you were meant for.

Think about it for a moment. What are your greatest strengths? If you have trouble identifying them, just think about what others say about you and your strengths. Sometimes others can see in you what you cannot. If you still need help, jump ahead to the Twenty-Four Character Strengths listed on page 90, and use those to help develop your list of top strengths.

Why is it so important that you begin thinking about your strengths right now? Your strengths have brought success in a variety of areas of your life. Your strengths define your character—who you are in good times and in bad. Unlike learned skills, your strengths come naturally. They are your areas of anointing, ways God has uniquely equipped you, so it makes sense that your load feels lighter when you put them to work.

For example, among my signature strengths are my faith and my sense of purpose. During some of the biggest challenges of my life—divorce (both my own and my parents'), the deaths of those close to me, the near death of my mother, my father's open-heart surgery, launching and running a business for fourteen years—my faith and my ability to see purpose in everything have given me the energy and guidance to persevere. I believe God is with me. So even when life isn't going the way I planned it, and even when plenty of reasons to doubt are all around me, I know the Lord is there. He speaks to me, especially when I quiet down enough to listen. When I silence my doubts, what bubbles up in my mind is a belief that God will give me the strength to handle whatever the enemy throws at me. I believe each difficult season serves to increase my resilience and perseverance because...*God says so:* "Consider it pure joy, my brothers and sisters, whenever you face trials of many kinds, because you know that the testing of your faith produces perseverance. Let perseverance finish its work so that you may be mature and complete, not lacking anything" (James 1:2–4).

Over time, my signature strengths have been nurtured through the trials of life. Indeed, I certainly wouldn't have felt led to write this book if not for the trials I have faced. They have expanded my faith and increased my compassion for those who face unexpected setbacks.

I can attest to the fact that the testing of your faith produces perseverance. As you go through your trial and eventually come out on the other side, you'll realize you can endure far more than you ever knew. You'll come to understand the depth of your faith and the magnitude of its strength. You can't come to that understanding apart from suffering. You may guess what you are capable of, but you don't actually know until you've been tested.

The challenges you face now are your test. And you will pass the test. I declare it right now through these pages: You will pass the test. You will endure. You will be better on the other side of this. You will have a testimony that blesses others and brings them closer to God. And you will do it using the personal strengths of character God has placed in you.

Think back to another time in your life when you conquered a challenge or persevered in the face of difficult odds. How did you do it? What strengths did you lean on to make it through?

What lessons from your past successes can empower you to persevere and succeed as you forge a new path for yourself now?

When you look back ten years from now, what will you want to be able to say about how you handled the challenge you currently face? And what strengths will you wish you had used?

Twenty-Four Character Strengths

Researchers led by Dr. Christopher Peterson at the University of Michigan have developed a list of twenty-four positive character strengths that are universally valued across world cultures.[5] Circle the top five or so that resonate with you—the traits that you celebrate, frequently use, and that fulfill and energize you. You might also ask one or two people who are very close to you to identify the five strengths they see in you.

- appreciation of beauty and excellence
- bravery and valor
- capacity to love and be loved
- caution, prudence, and discretion
- citizenship, teamwork, and loyalty
- creativity, ingenuity, and originality
- curiosity and interest in the world
- fairness, equity, and justice
- forgiveness and mercy
- gratitude
- honesty, authenticity, and genuineness
- hope, optimism, and future-mindedness
- humor and playfulness
- industry, diligence, and perseverance
- judgment, critical thinking, and open-mindedness
- kindness and generosity
- leadership
- love of learning
- modesty and humility
- perspective (wisdom)
- self-control and self-regulation
- social intelligence
- spirituality, sense of purpose, and faith
- zest, enthusiasm, and energy

To find out which ones really are your signature strengths, check out the assessment on the University of Pennsylvania positive psychology Web site, www.authentichappiness.com. It is free, but you will have to register on the Web site. The assessment will take you about forty minutes, and you'll be delighted to see your results.

Watch for Energy Drainers

As you work toward getting stabilized, one of your highest priorities is to conserve your energy for the things that matter. Give yourself the space you need to cope with your new reality. Anything that does not serve the purpose of lifting you up and moving you forward needs to fall to the bottom of your to-do list. In most cases, it needs to fall completely off your list of priorities until you have your bearings again. You cannot afford to invest your limited energy in dead ends.

Imagine four or five rescue workers standing above your ditch, prepared to pull you out. Each one lassos you with a rope, presumably working to gently lift you out of that deep hole. But as they begin to lift you up, each pulls in a different direction. Rather than lifting you up and out, they squeeze the life out of you as each rope works against the other. The same holds true when you give your energy to a variety of lesser priorities when a crisis demands your attention.

What aspects of your life are draining your energy? What squeezes the life out of you rather than gives you life? Whether it is a negative friend or the energy it takes to lead a local group in which you've been active, be realistic about what you can handle right now. Sometimes energy drains are subtle, such as the expectations of others that you simply cannot fulfill right now or destructive criticism you do not need to hear. Eliminating these energy guzzlers may take honest conversation, asking directly for what you want and need. And sometimes, it requires tough choices to protect your energy.

When Jeannette nearly failed out of college after her first year, her confidence took a hit, but she was determined to redeem herself. Yet when she returned for the fall semester of her sophomore year, she was still committed to the same social calendar that had contributed to her failings. Jeannette loved hanging out with her roommate, who had made the dean's list the previous year but was also involved in student government, intramural tennis, and attended every school football game.

By October, however, it became obvious that Jeannette couldn't participate in all those activities, hold down her job as a student assistant, and still achieve academic success. Reluctantly, she dropped all extracurricular activities except her part-time job. "It was a burden lifted," she says. "I had not even thought of it as a burden before I experienced what it was like to free up my time to focus on the top priority—getting back on track and *not* getting kicked out of school."

Identifying areas where you can cut back is key, but you'll also want to watch for ways to build up and conserve your physical, mental, and emotional energy, particularly if you're dealing with an ongoing challenge—a job loss, divorce, and problems with your health or your children, for example. Daily meditation, exercise, and restful sleep will all help you reduce stress and conserve your energy.

But even as you navigate these long-term challenges, the smaller daily challenges of life won't disappear. Things that you previously might have shrugged off, like a thoughtless or critical comment from a coworker, may threaten your hard-earned sense of optimism and peace. When you feel tempted to overreact in the heat of the moment, pause for a moment to give yourself a chance to regain your equilibrium. Whether it's taking a few deep breaths or a walk around the block, pausing before you react can defuse a situation, significantly reduce stress, and help you direct your energy toward taking positive steps forward.

In the future, when you look back on this challenging time in your life, how will you want to be able to say you approached it?

What actions or choices will empower you to approach your challenge in that way?

As you try to gain perspective on your situation, it can help to talk things through with a trusted person in your life. Discussing your situation with a friend or counselor can leave your spirits lighter and your head clearer about how to move forward. But choose your talking partner wisely; some friends will get you more worked up than you already are! And that's not good for your stress level. Choose someone who won't feed the fire of negative emotions, but instead will give you a helpful perspective and will encourage you to tackle the issue at hand in a wise way.

Who can best help you maintain a positive, productive outlook?

You Have Everything You Need

Use the Power of Your *Thoughts*

Use your thoughts to build your confidence by recalling your past victories. Reflect on what it took for you to succeed in the past. You have it in you to triumph in the face of your biggest setbacks. Remind yourself of what you are made of!

Use the Power of Your *Words*

Say it aloud: "With God, all things are possible. I have it within me to get through this and emerge a stronger and better person."

Use the Power of Your *Actions*

Today, start tapping into your strengths. Identify one way in which you will use your strengths to overcome a specific challenge you now face.

Use the Power of *Relationships*

Sometimes it can be hard to objectively evaluate your own strengths. Because they come so naturally, you may not even recognize them as special. Ask someone close to you to describe the strengths that really stand out in you.

Use the Power of *Prayer*

Lord, thank You for equipping me with everything I need to navigate the setbacks and unexpected turns in my life. Help me see the strengths You've placed in me and enable me to use them to move forward in a powerful way. Amen.

Triumph Over Trials: Faith's Story

In 1995, Faith Proietti discovered a lump in her breast—the first of three setbacks that changed her and her family forever.

"My grandmother had died of breast cancer, so I took that very seriously," she says. Faith went in the next day for a mammogram, which led to a biopsy. As she sat with her husband to await the results of her biopsy, her doctor, who was also a good friend, came around the corner with tears in his eyes. She knew immediately the results were not good. It was cancer. The doctor suggested she have a mastectomy the next week, followed by six months of chemotherapy.

"I was in shock," Faith remembers. "And I look over and my husband is sobbing. I'm wondering, *Why am I not crying? What's wrong with me?*" Reflecting back, she says that being blindsided by such news can feel surreal. "For the person it is hitting, I think it is a defense mechanism that keeps you together. If we take in all the information at once, it would be overwhelming and too hard to process," says Faith. "The numbness is like emotional padding. It keeps us sane."

But when reality finally set in, Faith grew frustrated, even angry. *Why me?* she wondered. "It took a long time to settle into it. Grief doesn't happen when you discover the diagnosis. You take it in mentally, but you haven't processed it spiritually or emotionally. There was a time of disorganization. I didn't know where I wanted to go from here. You begin to question who you are. There were times when I didn't want to look in the mirror. I didn't want to pray. There were times I didn't think there was anything to live for."

Ironically, just months before her diagnosis, Faith, a bereavement chaplain with a doctorate, had been hired to work for a local hospice. "I thought, *How am I ever going to help people who are terminally ill and here I have cancer?*" It was tough, but she says through her health challenge she became more compassionate toward the patients she served in her hospice work.

"I think when you work through your trial and you choose to respond with hope, to find purpose for it, you gain resilience for the next hurdle." Faith would certainly need that resilience for the next, more devastating challenge.

Faith's daughter, Lauren Kay, was eight at the time of her mother's diagnosis. A feisty kid, she was a leader in the Proietti family—a mediator of sorts who adored animals. Lauren had been born a month premature, and difficulties ensued soon after her birth. She stopped breathing at two weeks old—which launched an ongoing life-and-death battle. Faith and her husband, Rev. Gary Proietti, had to learn CPR. For more than a year, Lauren was on a monitor at night. "There would be two to five episodes per night in which she would stop breathing," Faith recalls. They would jump out of bed when the monitor sounded, administer CPR to get Lauren breathing again, and then attempt to go back to sleep. Of course, when your baby is struggling to breathe, sleep is hard to come by.

Then at two years old, Lauren fell out of bed, and the fall split her chin from ear to ear. "We thought, *This cannot be normal,*" Faith says. "We had two older kids, so we were not new parents." Lauren bruised easily, too. After a few years of medical tests, when Lauren was about six, they discovered that she had a connective tissue disorder called Ehlers-Danlos syndrome, Type IV. Her first cousin, Bryon, suffered from a similar but more severe disorder.

One night in November 1998, they noticed that Lauren's neck was swollen. "She was on antibiotics, so we thought it was related to the medicine." But at one o'clock that morning, she awoke in intense pain. They took Lauren to the hospital where Faith was working at the time.

The medical team discovered that the young girl's carotid artery was bleeding. To treat her, doctors gave Lauren medicine, which made her nauseous—and began a chain reaction. The nausea caused her to throw up, and the strain of throwing up caused the artery to burst, causing a massive stroke. "We brought her in at 1:30 a.m., and by 5 a.m., she was gone," Faith says.

"The day my daughter died, there was this deep, deep hole I felt in the middle of my chest. It was an emotional pain that stayed there for eight or nine months." She knew that if she didn't find a way to move forward, she too would die. *What right do I have to live?* she thought. *I gave birth to her and all this misery.* Faith knows her thoughts were absurd, but they were nonetheless destructive. "As parents, we have to forgive ourselves for all the things we wish we had done and didn't do." For example, Lauren had carried some boxes the day of her death. Faith worried that perhaps the load could have contributed to Lauren's pain that night. "You have to forgive yourself for what you didn't know," she says.

But such forgiveness doesn't come easily. Faith's turning point came in the form of a dream one morning after hitting the snooze button. She describes it this way:

In the dream, I heard my husband say, "Come on down and see the three kids." I was angry at him. Why would he say this? He knows Lauren is gone. I went down, and all three were sitting in rocking chairs. I said to Lauren, "What are you doing here? You're dead." She said, "I know. I came back to tell you something." She paused, and I noticed that her hair looked so clean and radiant. She said, "Mom, you have to let go. You have to let go of me." And I began to bawl. I said, "Lauren, you don't understand. I hurt so bad. I want you to be here." She said, "I know. But I am okay." I said, "How?" I just didn't know how to release her. She simply replied, "Let go."

In the dream, she gave me permission to let go. When she did, I chose to live. She said, "Mom, you have so much more to do. Don't let me keep you from doing it." With that, I put my head in my hands and sobbed some more. When I looked back up, Lauren was gone. My other two children, Valerie and Michael, were still there in their rocking chairs, but she was gone. This dream, this encounter, saved my life.

Before that day, Faith had beaten herself up, convinced she was a horrible mother because she never had dreams of Lauren. She says she even struggled to picture her daughter's face in her mind. "I would run to her picture and say to myself, *Why can't I see you?*" The dream allowed her to see Lauren one more time, and it helped her move on.

Crying and feeling depressed are not signs that you lack faith or that you are not resilient, Faith says. She cautions that sometimes clergy and well-meaning church members can do more harm than good in trying to reconcile our pain with their theology. The day after Lauren's funeral, Faith went into the hospital for an infection related to her mastectomy three years earlier. A minister who came into the room to "comfort" her said, "If you had just had enough faith, your daughter would have lived." Faith was so grateful that she had a deeper understanding of faith than to believe that. "You have to stand strong in your faith and not allow others' judgments to bring you down," she says.

When working with patients and families, Faith says, "I tell them God is crying with you. Jesus was a great example. Jesus *wept* when Lazarus died. He saw the pain and hurt. He didn't raise everyone from the dead who had died, but He had compassion."

Faith had to use her understanding of the Word when she faced yet a third crisis in five years. In 2000, the cancer returned. "I was more prepared the second time," she says. "It was hard. I had reached my five-year mark of being cancer-free and that is often a sign that it is gone for good." She underwent reconstruction, and even jokes now, "I don't have to wear a bra!"

Although she's been through a lot, Faith says she doesn't believe God causes tragedy in order to teach us lessons. "I believe as life unfolds, through the experiences and hurdles we face, we can choose to use that event in our life for good." It is Commitment #5 at work: I will choose to believe all things work together for good. "We choose whether it will destroy us or whether we will allow it to build us. It will create character and purpose and vision and compassion and a sense of empathy we would not have had."

In her work since the mid-1990s, Faith has ministered at over 350 funerals and says her experiences have pushed her to be the best chaplain she can be for the people she serves. "People tell me that when they look into my eyes, they see my love and care for them. I do what I do because I truly love."[6]

FAITH'S LESSONS FROM THE DITCH

- *Learn as much as you can so you can make good and healthy choices.* Learn as much as possible about your disease, divorce proceedings, what is needed to survive in your career industry—whatever touches your present challenge.

- *Be patient with yourself.* The moment-by-moment experiences create resilience. If you hurry yourself through it too quickly, instead of going at a pace that is comfortable for you, you won't receive the fullness of God's joy and healing. Be kind to yourself when you are going slower that you would like to.

- *Accept where you are.* Don't push yourself beyond where you need to go.
- *Get support.* There are other people going through what you are going through. Find them. Talk about it. Don't try to go through this alone.

SIX

Where Can You Turn for Help?

*Learning to Receive
with Grace and Humility*

Two years after losing her husband, Mike, to an aggressive form of cancer, Lori was recovering remarkably well. She'd allowed family and friends to give her the emotional and moral support she needed. She'd participated in a grief recovery group organized by her local hospital, which seemed to help her process her emotions as she mourned her loss alongside other people who were experiencing similar emotions.

But one thing provoked deep sadness and left Lori feeling overwhelmed: her "honey-do" list. A traditional husband, Mike had taken care of anything and everything that involved home repairs, cars, yard work, or negotiations of any kind. In nineteen years of

- *Identify your needs.*

- *Let go of your pride and ask for help.*

- *Seek professional support, if you need it.*

marriage, Lori never had to worry about taking out the trash, calling the plumber, getting the car repaired, or even washing her car. Handling those things was one of the ways Mike had loved and supported their family. But now he was gone, leaving Lori and their two teenaged girls to deal with all those tasks and more. It wasn't that any task was particularly hard; the problem was how it made her feel to have to do it all—alone. Each chore was a tangible symbol of her deeper losses: support, partnership, companionship, love.

When her friend Rita suggested that she ask some male family members to help with a few things—like trimming bushes or accompanying her to the car mechanic—Lori grew silent. She didn't like to ask for help. She didn't want anyone taking pity on her or feeling obligated to help indefinitely. But after the heat pump went out, the refrigerator began making a strange noise, and the basement flooded in an unusually heavy rainstorm—all in the space of a few days—Lori was overwhelmed. She swallowed her pride and phoned a handy cousin for help. To her surprise, he said he was honored that she had called. He'd wanted to help make her life a little easier. He knew Mike's death had been emotionally devastating for Lori and the girls, but Lori had always insisted everything was fine and she didn't need anything. The moment Lori heard her cousin's genuine response to her request, she felt relieved. Just knowing someone was available to help was comforting—and realizing that she only had to ask was empowering.

When we think of resilient people, we often think of the steely character who doesn't need anyone's help. He pulls himself up by his own bootstraps. No matter what happens, he has an answer for it. No matter how grim the circumstances, he is optimistic about the future. But when you face a big enough adversity, doubts will come. Some days you will feel like giving up. At times optimistic people or positive comments will only exasperate you, because all you can see is the magnitude of the mountain in front of you. You long for hope, but you keep feeling despair. You want to maintain a positive attitude, but you've been disappointed one too many times and you've started to feel like you're kidding yourself.

If you struggle with any of those thoughts, I have good news for you: it doesn't mean you're doing something wrong; it means you're human. Resilience is not about looking perfect or maintaining a flawlessly upbeat attitude as you navigate your way out of a ditch and onto a new path. What matters is that you climb out of that ditch, even if you occasionally stumble on your way up.

To be resilient, you've got to forgive your weaknesses and focus on your strengths; you've got to be flexible in seeing multiple ways out and smart enough to know you don't have to do it all on your own. In fact, you can't do it all on your own.

Calling for help

Remember Claire, the superwoman who lost her mother, her life savings, two jobs, and a marriage all in the span of a year? She said her turning point came when she fell to her knees in the kitchen and asked God why she had ended up in a marriage with an emotionally absent spouse during the worst period of her life. God simply told her He was with her and He would supply her needs.

Claire realized she couldn't lean on her own understanding or solve things with her own strength, but she was assured of God's love and peace in the midst of her setbacks. He was her first source of help. She needed emotional help. She needed financial help. And He met each and every need. "There were days when I didn't know how I would pay for lights, gas for my car so I could get to my mother's house, or even food," she says. "But every day, somehow, it would work out."

She learned just how literal God's promise was one summer evening right after her mother died. Despite the late hour, it was still over a hundred degrees in her southern town.

"It was about eight o'clock at night and the electricity went out," she remembers. Knowing she was late paying the bill, she checked to see if electricity was out on the whole street or if it was just their house. It was their house only. "We packed up and were prepared to go to my cousin's house," she says. "But before we could leave, miraculously, the lights came back on!" The electricity continued to run for two days until she was finally able to pay the bill. "After that, I just stopped worrying. I learned how to let go. I put it all in His hands. We never went hungry. We never went without anything we needed."

God's provision isn't always about supernatural blessings, though. Often, as you are on your journey of recovery, He will bless you through other people. That means accepting help. It can be difficult at times, especially when you have to accept assistance from those you've helped in the past.

Claire had always been the person in her family who provided financial, emotional, and spiritual support to others. So it was a new and humbling experience to ask for and accept help. "For the first time, I learned how to take, after years of being the giver for the whole family. It was very hard. For the first time in my entire life, I had to borrow money," she recalls. "When people offered, I had to take what they offered because I needed it."

She remembers how her uncle had bought extra toilet paper and toiletries at Sam's Club because he knew how tight money was for her. When he offered these basic provisions, she wanted to decline but couldn't afford to. She needed what he was giving her.

Depending on others can leave you feeling vulnerable, but to get out of the ditch, you'll have to let go of pride and accept the blessing of help.

Resilience isn't about going it alone. While we live in a very individualistic culture, no one succeeds by doing it all on her own.

After Kevin Wolitzky became paralyzed at age eighteen, accepting help was an essential part of making his way to a new path in life. "When you are disoriented and you stand up in that ditch, you need to find something you can focus on and rely on that's always going to be there," he says. "For me, it was family and friends. I had to lean on them real hard for a while. That was new for me and it was hard, but I had to."

Resilient People Know . . .

You can get by with a little help from your friends, just as the Beatles sang. Research shows that people who have at least three or four very close friends have higher well-being—in other words, a more satisfying quality of life derived from a combination of healthy relationships, loving what you do each day, and good physical and financial health.[1]

MYTH VERSUS TRUTH

Why is it so difficult to accept help when we really need it? Maybe because many of us have a skewed perspective about this subject.

Let's look at some of the most common myths about needing help, and the truth that disputes each one.

Myth 1: Admitting I Need Help Shows a Lack of Faith
Truth: Needing help means you are willing to lean on God, who told the apostle Paul, "My grace is sufficient for you, for my power is made perfect

in weakness" (2 Corinthians 12:9). When you acknowledge your need for help, you recognize that you are human, and as a human, you are not all powerful. But God is. He is best able to demonstrate His power when you are least able to demonstrate yours.

Myth 2: I Should Be Able to Do Everything on My Own

Truth: God created us as interdependent beings, and the presence and help of others is a blessing.

> *Two are better than one,*
> > *because they have a good return for their labor:*
> *If either of them falls down,*
> > *one can help the other up.*
> *But pity anyone who falls*
> > *and has no one to help them up.*
> *Also, if two lie down together, they will keep warm.*
> > *But how can one keep warm alone?*
> *Though one may be overpowered,*
> > *two can defend themselves.*
> *A cord of three strands is not quickly broken.*
> > *(Ecclesiastes 4:9–12)*

Myth 3: I Shouldn't Bother Anyone Else with My Problems

Truth: Jesus Himself instructed us to come forward with our needs:

Ask and it will be given to you; seek and you will find; knock and the door will be opened to you. For everyone who asks receives; the one who seeks finds; and to the one who knocks, the door will be opened. Which of you, if your son asks for bread, will give him a stone? Or if he asks for a fish, will give him a snake? If you, then, though you are evil, know how to give good gifts to your children, how much more will your Father in heaven give good gifts to those who ask him! (Matthew 7:7–11)

Reading that scripture should be inspiration enough to ask for exactly what you need from the Lord! Recognize that His answer may be that it's time to ask someone for help. Asking is not bothersome; it is proactive. It is a belief that the right answer is out there. You just have to ask the right person. Pray for the discernment to do exactly that.

Myth 4: Smart People Can Figure Out the Answers on Their Own

Truth: Sometimes in life, intelligence is not going to get you what you need. In fact, intelligent people often get so used to relying on only themselves that they unconsciously start to believe they are godlike, that they know the answer for everything. Proverbs 12:15 cautions, "The way of fools seems right to them, but the wise listen to advice." If you're truly intelligent, you'll recognize the benefits of a fresh perspective and practical help from those God directs you to seek out.

Myth 5: If I Need Help, I Have Completely Lost Control

Truth: You were never totally in control. You have some control—and it is wise to do all you can to positively impact your future—but life includes many factors beyond your control. When we get knocked into the ditch, the limitations of our power become clear. "Many are the plans in a person's heart, but it is the LORD's purpose that prevails" (Proverbs 19:21). Remember the Serenity Prayer, which talks about having the wisdom to accept what you can't change and the courage to change what you can? It applies here. One thing that definitely lies within your control is making the decision to ask for help—and having the humility to receive it with grace and gratitude.

CHOOSING TO RECEIVE

When we're in the position of giving, we typically do so by choice, which enhances our sense of being in control. But the dynamic shifts completely when we receive help, admitting that we're reliant on God and on others. With that admission sometimes comes a loss of confidence, a drop in our sense of self-worth—unless we choose to see it differently.

By shifting your perspective you can view help as a sign of God's favor on your life. He is providing for you during a time when you need extra assistance. I say "extra" because we always need help. You were being helped before your setback. You may not have seen it that way, but someone chose to show you favor by hiring you for your position or by patronizing your business. Certain aspects of your prior financial and personal success were directly connected to the favorable choices of others, whether or not you were aware of their decisions. In addition, God favored you with whatever level of strength and health you've enjoyed up to this point in life.

Your many accomplishments and victories prior to your setback were not achieved solely through your own strength. Activities occurred behind the scenes, others helped you in ways you will never be aware of, God orchestrated His purposes—all of which contributed to your progress in immeasurable ways.

So now is not the time to protect your pride but to seek God's favor and the support of others. "You have to humble yourself to ask for help," Kevin points out in describing those first months and years after becoming a quadriplegic. "Or at least be willing to receive help when it's offered. At times, I felt like I went back to being a baby."

Humility is a virtue God expects of us. And He often uses our setbacks to nurture this characteristic in our lives. Consider just a few of the places in the Bible that highlight the significance of humility and the danger of pride.

> When pride comes, then comes disgrace, but with humility comes wisdom. (Proverbs 11:2)

> Therefore, whoever takes the lowly position of this child is the greatest in the kingdom of heaven. (Matthew 18:4)

> God opposes the proud but shows favor to the humble. (James 4:6; 1 Peter 5:5)

> Humble yourselves, therefore, under God's mighty hand, that he may lift you up in due time. (1 Peter 5:6)

> Before a downfall the heart is haughty, but humility comes before honor. (Proverbs 18:12)

> Pride goes before destruction, a haughty spirit before a fall. (Proverbs 16:18)

Remember that, as you navigate the unexpected turn your life has taken, you will expend a great deal of energy managing your emotions and your reactions to the challenges you face. Your emotions and reactions are fed by your thoughts—how you interpret what is happening in your world. If you interpret your need for help in a negative way, your emotions and reactions will be counterproductive. If you buy into cultural myths about what it means to need help, you will find it harder to receive what you need and perhaps even fail to embrace the blessings God offers.

By contrast, if you view help from a positive perspective—as a tool and a resource to help you recover—then your emotions and reactions will be productive. Your burden becomes lighter as you reach out to others who can share their strength and resources with you.

In what way(s) do you need to ask for and/or receive help from others right now? Think about not only your concrete needs—such as transportation, groceries, help with housework—but also about less tangible needs. Perhaps you need emotional support to deal with the pain and loss you're experiencing. Maybe you need social support to remind you that you're not alone. Or maybe you need spiritual support—someone to pray with you or a place to fellowship with like-minded people.

Who do you know who could help with each of these needs—or has already offered to do so?

How do you feel about asking for that help? How will you feel when you receive that help?

If you are experiencing negative emotions or resistance about asking for help or receiving it, acknowledge those feelings and record your reasons for hesitation.

What would it take for you to work through those feelings and ask for the help you need?

As you work through these questions and craft a plan for seeking support and assistance, please keep in mind the three key aspects of getting the help you need:

1. Asking for help
2. Asking for the right kind of help
3. Asking the right person to help

If you ask prayerfully, you'll find guidance in all three of these areas. Asking for help requires humility. Asking for the right kind of help requires wisdom. Asking the right person to help requires discernment. Pray for all three, claiming the words of this psalm for your own life:

I lift up my eyes to the mountains—
*   where does my help come from?*
My help comes from the LORD,
*   the Maker of heaven and earth.*

He will not let your foot slip—
     he who watches over you will not slumber;
indeed, he who watches over Israel
     will neither slumber nor sleep.

*The L*ORD *watches over you—*
     *the L*ORD *is your shade at your right hand;*
the sun will not harm you by day,
     nor the moon by night.

*The L*ORD *will keep you from all harm—*
     he will watch over your life;
*the L*ORD *will watch over your coming and going*
     both now and forevermore. (Psalm 121:1–8)

A WORD OF CAUTION

When it comes to dealing with our challenges, there is such a thing as getting too much help. When you find yourself relinquishing your own power and allowing others to take over your life or you stop relying on God and turn first to people for help, it is likely you have crossed from healthy humility into dangerous dependence. And as much as someone may want to help, if you demand too much help from one friend or family member, that person may get burned out. That is why it's usually a good idea to rely on a team of people who can work from their individual strengths while being part of a common effort. One may be better at listening or giving wise counsel, while another person is great at the practical stuff, such as helping you revise your resume, assisting financially, baby-sitting for a few hours, or taking you to an appointment.

Sometimes, the problem is not about your overburdening someone with your need for support but about others burdening you with their need to help. When you go through a setback, some loved ones will over-react. They will insist on helping you in ways you may not need or want. Even if you do need the help, you may not feel this is the right person to provide it.

How do you say no when someone offers unneeded or unwanted help? Though it may feel ungrateful to refuse a gift, if you don't muster the courage to communicate, you may find yourself in an unnecessarily stressful situation. Here are some phrases you can use to speak up for yourself:

"I really appreciate your offer to help, but I want to handle this myself. I believe I can do it and I need to try."

"If I'm going to get through this, I'll have to do some things for myself. I need to get used to that."

"Thank you so much for your offer, but [Name] is helping me with that already."

If a person is persistent and ignores your decline of help, you can say: "I know you feel differently from the way I do, but I'm asking you to please respect my wishes on this."

WHEN YOU NEED PROFESSIONAL HELP

You may already have sought counseling or therapy to deal with the challenges you're facing, and if so, I want to acknowledge your wisdom in reaching out for help. In some communities, professional counseling is marred by an unfortunate and unfounded stigma, which can be downright harmful to those who most need healing. It is interesting that most people expect you to go see a doctor for any physical pain or trauma you encounter. The doctor might decide you need physical therapy, surgery, or some other treatment to help you heal and recover. But when you suffer emotional pain or trauma, you are somehow expected to face your challenges without getting a professional opinion or professional guidance for the best way to heal, recover, or navigate your situation.

Please don't let the opinions of others limit your options for seeking help. If you are experiencing symptoms of depression or you find yourself stuck and unable to move forward, please seek the help of a professional. If for any reason you're reluctant to seek treatment, talk to a friend or loved one, a health-care professional, a minister, or someone else you trust.

The Mayo Clinic warns of the following signs of depression.[2] Circle all that apply to you:

- Feelings of sadness or unhappiness
- Irritability or frustration, even over small matters
- Loss of interest or pleasure in normal activities
- Reduced sex drive
- Insomnia or excessive sleeping
- Changes in appetite—depression often causes decreased appetite and weight loss, but in some people it causes increased cravings for food and weight gain
- Agitation or restlessness—for example, pacing, hand wringing, or an inability to sit still
- Slowed thinking, speaking, or body movements
- Indecisiveness, distractibility, and decreased concentration
- Fatigue, tiredness, and loss of energy—even small tasks may seem to require a lot of effort
- Feelings of worthlessness or guilt, fixating on past failures or blaming yourself when things aren't going right
- Trouble thinking, concentrating, making decisions, and remembering things

- Frequent thoughts of death, dying, or suicide
- Crying spells for no apparent reason
- Unexplained physical problems, such as back pain or headaches

Particularly if you experience these symptoms for three weeks or longer, make an appointment with your doctor or with a mental-health professional as soon as possible. Depression symptoms might not get better on their own and, if untreated, may become worse. Serious depression can lead to suicidal thoughts and should be taken extremely seriously. If you or someone you know is having suicidal thoughts, *get help immediately*. Here are some steps you can take:

- Contact a family member or friend.
- Contact a counselor, doctor, minister, or some other health-care professional.
- Call a local suicide hot line—or you can use the toll-free, 24/7 hot line of the National Suicide Prevention Lifeline at 800-273-8255 to talk to a trained counselor.

The key is to reach out. If your emotions become too much to handle, stop trying to handle them all on your own. Again, reaching out is an important skill for nurturing resilience in difficult times.

You do not have to go through your challenge alone. In fact, one potential benefit of a major life challenge is that it holds the power to deepen your relationships in a way that the more trivial, everyday interactions of life cannot. When you look back years from now, you will see the power of positive relationships during this pivotal time in your life.

Reach out. It may be one of the most important steps you will take on this journey.

You Have Everything You Need

Use the Power of Your *Thoughts*
What myths have you bought into when it comes to asking for help? What truths will you adopt to counter those lies?

Use the Power of Your *Words*
Use the power of your words to ask for help—today. Ask graciously and receive gratefully.

Use the Power of Your *Actions*
Just because you need help doesn't mean you are not also in a position to help others. It is tremendously empowering to give what you also need. Who do you know who needs encouragement? Reach out and encourage someone else.

Use the Power of *Relationships*
Do everything in a spirit of love. Even in those times when you are frustrated or angry about your situation, choose to respond lovingly to those you encounter.

Use the Power of *Prayer*
Lord, as much as I sometimes hate to admit, I need help. I need Your help. And I need the help of other people as I navigate my way through the setbacks and unexpected turns in my life. Help me to embody the humility I need to ask for help, the discernment to know whom to ask, and the wisdom to know what to ask for. Amen.

Triumph Over Trials: Richard's Story

Richard had been in the media business for as long as he could remember. He began in radio, then transitioned to television, where for thirty-one years he worked behind the scenes as a cameraman, floor director, and then producer. "I love broadcasting," he says. "Even after more than three decades, I jumped out of bed in the morning, happy to go to work." So when he fell victim to a massive layoff by the parent company of his television station, he took the news especially hard. While some people see a layoff as a blessing in disguise to get them off the wrong path and onto the right one, Richard firmly believed he was already on the right path.

"I knew right away I had a big problem on my hands," he says. "At fifty-eight years old, it's tough to find work anywhere, but especially in media. It's a young person's industry. Sure, there are a lot of seasoned veterans out there, but they tend to be seasoned because they stayed in one place for a long time, like I did." He immediately set out to find a new job. "I followed all the advice you hear: reach out to colleagues and friends, have a professional write your resume, get out there and meet people," he says. "But the fact was, my company wasn't the only one struggling. Many in my area were scaling back, and when they hired new people, they tended to have twenty-five to thirty years less work experience because the companies are looking to keep salaries low."

As time went by and no strong job opportunities developed, Richard and his wife, Marie, soon went through his three-month severance package as well as the six-month emergency fund they'd saved. Marie's work as a receptionist brought in about a third of Richard's previous salary. She simply could not pay the bills they'd accumulated. The house they lived in was just five years old and carried a hefty mortgage. As months passed, they fell behind in their payments. Seeing no other option, they tapped their retirement savings. "We were thankful we had something more to tap into, but at our age, depleting your retirement fund just to pay the mortgage is really scary," he says. "I mean, we don't have thirty years to replenish that money."

Things continued to get worse. Marie lost her job when her employer replaced the receptionist position with an automated system as a cost-cutting measure. In the end, the couple lost their home, their life savings, and both of their jobs. But now Richard says that he is amazed by what they've gained along the way.

"After we lost our home, we downsized and got an apartment while I continued to look for work," he explains. "Freelance projects and temp assignments seemed to show up for one of us or the other just in the nick of time. All the while, we started to notice that despite all the financial turmoil and the lack of steady work, we were still pretty happy." Richard says they'd had "too much stuff." They had not thought of themselves as materialistic, but now that they'd shed so much space, they sold much of their furniture rather than paying for a bigger apartment or storage unit to house it. "We didn't lose family. We didn't go hungry. We had each other. We knew a breakthrough had to happen at some point, but we chose to be grateful that our problems were solvable. This would not ruin us."

Richard continued to look for a job, but the opportunities for him in Washington DC, seemed to be nearly nonexistent. Though they'd made their home in the same area for thirty-five years, they realized that bouncing back might mean being flexible enough to uproot and start over. So he began looking beyond the local area.

One day, Richard connected online with a colleague from his old job. "I mentioned my dilemma. I told him everything—about downsizing, losing the house, going through our savings. I wasn't trying to save my pride. I needed someone to help me, and sometimes you need people to understand the urgency of your situation. I didn't beg him for help. I just made it clear that if he could open doors anywhere in the country, I would be grateful." That's just what happened. Two years after Richard's layoff, his friend made a connection that led Richard to land a job in Florida working for a communications company.

Today he uses his broadcasting skills and mentors new talent. "I love my new job. It's something new. I love the people. And the weather is fantastic," Richard says. "Marie and I have a totally different outlook on life. The experience was stressful and we lost a lot, but we didn't lose our marriage. Our health is good, and we are bouncing back financially."

Richard admits to having felt depressed during one period of his unemployment, but he says putting things in perspective helped him climb out of that ditch. "It's all about how you think about what happens to you. You can either interpret it as the end of the world or the beginning of an adventure that may land you in a better spot than you imagined."[3]

RICHARD'S LESSONS FROM THE DITCH

- *Brace yourself for the long haul.* Sometimes you can get out of the ditch quickly, but sometimes it takes awhile. You have to be patient and believe things will work out eventually. If you get impatient, you only cause yourself more stress.

- *Look for the lesson.* We learned a really valuable lesson from our experience. It has changed how we value the "stuff" in our lives—whether nice cars, a big house, even gadgets and other things we spent money on before my layoff. Now, I really value my money in a whole new way. I don't just throw it away on things that don't have real meaning to me and my family.

- *Don't let pride get in the way of asking for help.* If not for reaching out to my old co-worker and telling him the real deal about how dire our financial situation was, I don't think we'd be where we are right now. You don't have to sound pitiful, but be honest. When you tell the truth, people are moved by it. We are so used to pretending we're okay even when we're not. Don't do that.

SEVEN

Where Will You Go from Here?

*Deciding Whether to Forge a New Path
or Return to the Old One*

U p to this point, we've been working to get you out of the ditch and back on your feet. Now, having dealt honestly with the questions so far, I believe you're fully prepared—mentally, emotionally, and spiritually—to tackle the key question each of us must face when life doesn't go according to plan... Where will I go from here?

You may not know the exact answer in this moment, but I believe the answer is on its way. Your job is to listen for it. You must trust and believe that, no matter what your answer, "all things work together for good to those who love God, to those who are the called according to *His* purpose" (Romans 8:28, NKJV).

- *Seek divine direction.*

- *Assess the benefits and drawbacks of paths, old and new.*

- *Map out a clear vision of where you want to go.*

But you need to know that no shortcut exists for crafting your come-back plan. You may be tempted to look to others for the answers, to get clues from other people's situations, or to do what everyone else is telling you to do. Please don't make this mistake.

Your primary guidance for where to go from here must come from within—from God's direction spoken into your heart. God speaks to you directly through the power of the Holy Spirit. Yes, He may speak through others to offer counsel for your situation and confirm His leading, but He will not bypass you. Ask Him for wisdom as you answer the critical questions about how to move forward from here. James 1:5 promises, "If any of you lacks wisdom, you should ask God, who gives generously to all without finding fault, and it will be given to you."

GETTING BACK ON TRACK— OR CHOOSING A NEW DESTINATION

The first critical decision to make is whether you will continue toward the destination you had in mind before life knocked you off course, or whether it's time to forge a new path altogether. While the simplest solution may appear to be getting your life back on track just as quickly as possible and making up for lost time, that may not be the right choice for you.

Your setback offers an opportunity you may not otherwise have had—or at least could not have pursued as easily. For example, a year ago maybe you came up with a terrific idea for a creative service no one else is offering—but you chose not to follow through. Though you weren't crazy about your job, you had no intention of giving up a steady salary to start a new business. Such a venture just seemed too risky. But once you've been laid off and no longer have a paycheck to lose, you may realize you've been set free to pursue your entrepreneurial dreams.

On the other hand, getting knocked off your path doesn't necessarily mean you aren't supposed to be on it. Maybe the job you lost could have been the perfect career path for you and you should strive to get a similar position. If so, then you'll want to devise a plan to make a comeback—and bring with you the lessons you've learned to make you stronger this time around. Or maybe your setback was relational. You encountered a serious roadblock—a betrayal of some sort or your spouse's admission of an affair. But you are convinced God wants you to work through it, to repair what's been broken by the betrayal as well as to resolve any other issues that may have contributed to it. You're not going to forge a new path by ending the relationship; instead, you'll pursue your same goal of a healthy marriage while determining what course corrections will help you avoid a repeat incident.

Even if your vision for the impacted area of your life remains unchanged and you want to pursue the same destination as before, you may realize that other aspects of your life are screaming for change. A setback gives you the opportunity to reevaluate life at every level—your career choices, where you live, how you live, your financial goals, your personal priorities, and your relationship choices. Certainly, if your setback was health related, such as suffering a heart attack, your hope is to restore your physical health—but that may require some significant changes in your diet and exercise habits, which may reshape how you use your time. Perhaps you'll want to consider moving closer to your parents, who are willing to help with your children, thereby strengthening your support structure and reducing your stress.

Keep in mind that even if you have the same goals as before your setback, you may need to find a new way of reaching them. For example, Tracy and Nick tried for six years to conceive a child, but they experienced one disappointment after another. Tracy became pregnant early on but lost the baby. In the years to follow, she never became pregnant again, despite numerous fertility treatments. But this resilient couple didn't give up on their dream of becoming parents. They chose a new path: adoption. This path too brought some disappointments. On two occasions, they thought they had a new baby, only to have their expectations dashed when the birth mother changed her mind. But they held out hope for the baby God meant for them. It turns out, God intended two children for Tracy and Nick. They brought home three-week-old twins, Abigail and Amy, three years after they set out on the path to adoption. It wasn't the path they had originally envisioned, but in their words, "These are the children we were meant to parent."

Be open to new options. Rather than forging ahead on your old trail, you may need to blaze a new one.

SEEKING DIVINE DIRECTION

Your decision about where to go from here begins with getting divine direction. Hearing God's voice is essential to determining your best next step. I believe He is speaking to you right now. Sometimes His voice speaks loud and clear through the circumstances of our lives. Other times, we must quiet ourselves to listen for that still small voice that says either, *"It's time for a change"* or *"Stick with it. Push through. Now is not the time to give up."*

Only you can know how God is directing you. You must trust and believe that while God sometimes offers confirmation through others, He speaks to you directly too. He will give you peace about the direction you should go. He will direct your steps. Consider the promise of Proverbs 3:5–6:

Trust in the LORD with all your heart,
And lean not on your own understanding;

In all your ways acknowledge Him,
      And He shall direct your paths. (NKJV)

So we have instruction about how to obtain God's direction for the path we should take. First, trust Him. That's not always as easy as it sounds. Although we want to believe that He'll work everything out for our good, most of us find it difficult to release control and live in the uncertainty of the in-between time. We look at our current circumstances and have trouble envisioning a time of blessing beyond the pain of now. And that's exactly why the second part of the passage reminds us not to lean on our own understanding.

The third segment of the verse points to one of the best ways to build our trust in God: acknowledge Him. Acknowledge His wisdom and power. Acknowledge that He is in control even when it doesn't seem that way. Acknowledge all that He has already done for you. As you notice the abundant blessings you have experienced and indeed are experiencing right now, it becomes easier to believe that He can bless you again, even more abundantly.

God Brought You This Far

A routine physical exam at age fifty-five led to a startling discovery for my father. Noticing that his heartbeat appeared to be irregular, the doctor ordered further tests. I went to the hospital with Dad on the day of the angiogram, a test typically used to determine if the arteries are blocked. This seemed unlikely, because my father has always been slim, and since retiring from the Air Force after more than twenty-four years of service, he has remained healthy and active in his second career.

After the angiogram was complete, the doctor called me in to join them as he discussed the test results with Dad. He began with, "We have some good news and some bad news." This is never a statement you want to hear from a doctor. "The good news," he continued, "is that your arteries are in perfect condition. No blockages whatsoever."

Dad and I looked at each other in nervous relief, glad to know he wouldn't need any stents but anxious about what news the doctor would share next.

"The bad news is that one of your arteries is going to the wrong place, and the other artery has grown to three and a half times the normal size to compensate." He paused before continuing, "It is a very rare birth defect that would normally have taken your life by the time you were six months old. Honestly, I have never seen anyone live to your age with this condition uncorrected. You could walk up and down the streets of New York City all day long and you wouldn't find anyone else with this problem. It happens, but it is highly unusual."

I tried to hide how shaken and scared this news had left me because I wanted to be strong for my dad. But if he was in shock, he certainly didn't show it. After processing the information for a minute, he asked calmly, "So can anything be done about it?"

The doctor said, "Yes, we recommend corrective open-heart surgery. We can take an artery from your leg and 'rewire your plumbing' so to speak. We recommend you have surgery immediately."

Whoa, I thought. *Did he just say open-heart surgery?* I felt sick. Just five years earlier, my mother had suffered a massive brain aneurysm while we were talking on the phone. She'd had emergency brain surgery as a result, and her physical recovery is still a work in progress. Now my dad needed heart surgery?

My thoughts went straight to concern for his survival. *Will he live through it? Even if it's successful, does this mean his life expectancy will be shorter?* My mind would have churned out fifty more anxiety-producing questions if my father hadn't interrupted.

"So, it's a miracle I'm alive?" he asked.

The doctor smiled slightly.

"Well," Dad continued. "I don't think God has brought me this far just to take me now."

For more than half a century, God had kept my dad's heart pumping when medical science says he should have died long ago. By acknowledging the magnitude of the blessing that had kept him alive for fifty-five years, my father found confidence to trust God to produce one more miracle: a successful surgery. Three weeks later, I watched Dad smile and crack jokes as nurses wheeled him off to open-heart surgery. He trusted the Lord that everything would be all right. And it was.

Put Your Trust into Practice

What about you? Does the challenge confronting you right now seem too big for God? Nothing is impossible with Him. You have an opportunity right now to exercise trust on a higher level than you ever have before. That trust begins by noticing and acknowledging all that He has already done. The ditch you landed in could have been much deeper but for the grace of God. Trust Him to do great things. It's the first step to getting direction from Him.

Let's be clear though: trusting isn't about clinging blindly to the outcome you want. It's about asking God to show you the next step, to help you discover where to go from here—even if you *don't* get the outcome for which you prayed. Some aspects of your life may never return to normal, at least not "normal" as you knew it before you landed in the ditch. Will you trust God fully and go with His plan even if you don't understand it? Will you refuse to rely on your own understanding? Will you acknowledge Him? If you answer yes to these three questions, Proverbs 3:5–6 promises He will direct your paths.

With that in mind, it's time to tackle the question of where you will go from here. Let's begin with any divine nudges you may sense in your spirit.

What do you sense God is telling you about where you should go from here? Is He telling you to get back to your old path as soon as you can? Or is He nudging you toward something new or different—a new career path, a move to a new city, or a change in your lifestyle habits? Record what you're hearing from Him.

If you're not sure if or what God has said on the matter, what inklings do you have about how to move forward? Acknowledge here any ideas or thoughts that have come to you, no matter how random. Be honest.

If you believe that God may be calling you to persevere on the old path, consider the following questions:

- What will you gain by returning to the old path? What would you lose by pursuing a new direction in this area of life?

- Is a return to your old path truly within your control? What would it require of you?

- What reservations do you have about trying to move forward on the same path? What excites you about continuing on in the same direction?

Forging a New Path

Many people will see their setback merely as an unexpected twist or temporary delay along the path they were meant to travel. But in my coaching and my personal experience, I've found that just as often these jolts serve to send people in new directions.

Even if you see some benefits in pursuing the same old path, you may decide it's not for you. *Why go back there? It wasn't my ideal circumstance anyway,* you conclude. *This is my chance to make some adjustments, start over and pursue the path that's truly meant for me. It's a second chance.*

But in many instances, the decision to forge a new path is not really about seizing a second chance to pursue the desires of your heart. Instead, it's based on the reality that your old path is no longer an option. Perhaps your health has been irreparably damaged, your marriage has ended through divorce or death, or you've lost your home to foreclosure. What-ever the situation, you know that the old route to the life you hoped for has been permanently closed.

Right now it may seem as if the power to choose has been snatched away from you, but please know that you are still very much in control of how you will respond. You can allow a new path to be thrust upon you— or you can be proactive and chart a new course intentionally. If this is your predicament, I invite you to choose the latter. Be intentional. Muster the courage to persevere through the pain and disappointment. Design this next stage of your life believing that something good lies ahead. Even the worst of setbacks brings the opportunity for positive change. You may discover new purpose in your life. You may one day look back to realize that the end of your dream marked the beginning of something fresh and unexpected and beautiful.

Resilient People Know . . .

Research shows positive emotion opens the mind and improves decision making.[1] Have a good laugh or do something for fun before you start writing your vision.

Consider the Big Picture

Whatever the circumstances, now that you're no longer focused on your previous path, you have an opportunity to look out from the mountain-top and find your authentic path. A whole new set of opportunities has opened up to you. Your options have expanded, and you have the chance to realign your life to reflect your core values and passions. That's exactly what happened in my case.

As I evaluated my best next step after my divorce, I found that doing so involved many layers of decisions. For example, I had moved to Maryland for that marriage, but now that my reason for living there had disappeared, would I remain in the area or build my new life elsewhere? And if I left, where would I go? At this critical moment, I stepped back to take a look at the big picture of my life.

I pondered this question: *Is there something I have wanted but never had?* That brought to mind my dreams of doing television and media at a higher level. In the previous couple of years, I had been contacted about several opportunities that would expand my platform, but they were always in one of two places: New York or Los Angeles. I wondered if I should consider starting over in one of these cities. Both sounded exciting. But I was surprised that the idea of moving to either location brought a feeling of sadness. I sensed this meant that neither was the right direction for me at this point, but I didn't know why.

As you consider what path to pursue, pay attention to the emotions that surface as you contemplate your options. Listen to those feelings and consider what they might be trying to tell you. God gifts us with both positive and negative emotions for a purpose. Our job is to use those emotions to guide us toward His will. Emotions carry messages that can teach us crucial insights about ourselves and help us navigate the landscape of our lives. In my book *What's Really Holding You Back?* I share an entire chart of negative emotions and the corresponding message each sends.[2] Sadness—the feeling that took me by surprise as I considered moving to a place such as New York—usually indicates that we feel a sense of loss.

Emotions can even help us understand the purpose behind choosing one path over another. It isn't enough to know what *not* to choose—for example, not choosing to move to New York. Knowing why you are not choosing it can give you clues about what *to* choose.

What loss was prompting the feeling of sadness when I thought of New York or Los Angeles? Each time I thought of those cities, I could see my mother's face. My brother's face. Then I began to see various members of my large extended family—all of whom live far away from those two cities. Understanding the reason for my sadness not only told me what not to choose but also gave me new insight into what I really did want. This is when the real soul searching began.

I love family. If there is one place I have consistently felt contentment, joy, and freedom, it is in the presence of my family. But in the first thirty-six years of my life, I nearly always lived far from them—in Florida, Germany, Colorado, California, Texas, and then Maryland. Though I spent many childhood summers in my parents' hometown in South Carolina, growing up in a military family meant we always lived elsewhere. Then as an adult, I had continued to live far from my extended family.

The answer to my question, "Where will I go from here?" was becoming clearer, but I wanted to be sure. I closed my eyes in prayer, and an image came to me. I could see a map of the United States and God's hand waiting for me to land in His palm in the southeast corner of that map. I felt a gentle pull south and perceived I would feel centered and grounded there. I sensed it would be a soft, welcoming landing in an area I considered home because it is where most of my entire family lives—between Atlanta and the Carolinas. As I weighed the idea, I felt peace, relief, and excitement—a sense of brightness in the darkness of starting my life over. And those emotions—peace, relief, and excitement—made clear the desires of my heart and confirmed God's direction.

Going south felt right, but where exactly? In that moment I learned another important lesson about making decisions after a setback: you don't have to have all the answers. Sometimes, simply giving yourself the space to transition in baby steps will empower you to get your bearings and ultimately discover the bigger steps that will come later.

My baby step was moving temporarily to Anderson, South Carolina, which gave me time to process what was happening in my life before making decisions about where to live. For three months, I enjoyed the company of my mother and my much younger brother. I spent time with family, attended a church founded and led by my aunt and uncle, and began walking every morning—sometimes with family members. I found joy in the midst of my pain, and the next step—making my home permanently in the southeast—was unmistakable.

What Are You Hearing?

Forging a new path takes courage and boldness. It takes decisiveness. But most of all it requires confidence that this path will lead toward God's greater purposes for your life. I believe you have it within you to blaze a new trail if that's what God is calling you to do. The following self-coaching questions will help you gain clarity on what your new path may look like.

Do you sense God pulling you onto a new path? Explain your answer.

What emotion(s) do you feel as you ponder the possibility of a new path? What message is each emotion offering you?

If God were sitting next to you right now, what would He tell you about what path to take?

Capture a Clear Vision

Today you have the opportunity for a new beginning. Your setback can turn into your setup for something good that is to come. What initially appears to be an obstacle can actually reposition you for a new season of life—one that is richer and more rewarding than what you might have otherwise experienced. It is your choice whether to forge ahead with joy and vision or to plod onward with dread and indecision.

Remember Faith Proietti, the mother and chaplain who was diagnosed with an advanced stage of breast cancer? Her vision was to help people as a chaplain. She believes she has carried out that vision with far more compassion because she has twice experienced cancer. "I was really able to put my arms around my clients and love them with a compassion I would not have, had I not gone through having cancer," she says. "I have done over 350 funerals in the last seventeen years. It has pushed me to be the best chaplain and minister for my clients that I can be."

If the unexpected twist in your life is temporary, such as a job loss or financial challenge, this may be your opportunity to completely change directions and revamp some aspect of your life. If this is the case for you, be thankful for your setback! It is a chance to say, "Now that change has been thrust upon me, let me do what I really wanted to do anyway!" or "I'm ready to try something new. This is my chance to go for it!"

Even if you're dealing with a permanent change or irreversible loss, you still need a vision of where you're going and how you want to live life on this new path. What purpose will you glean from your pain? What level of faith and hope do you want to show to the world? Will you be a victim or will you be victorious?

Lillian Sparks, whom you met earlier, watched in distress as the nurses wheeled her newborn child into her hospital room in an incubator. Every time he kicked or moved, his little body endured fresh pain from the balloonlike blisters all over his body. But in that moment Lillian's husband reminded her of the prayer for their future in ministry the couple had prayed while they were engaged: "Lord, we want our anointing to be different. We will do whatever it takes."

They decided that day to do whatever it took to love and care for Bryon. "We said, *We accept this as his parents, as part of Your will for our lives,*" Lillian recalls. "I believed that what the enemy meant for evil, God meant for good."

This young couple, just twenty-two years old and new to the ministry—but mature in faith—created a vision for their life with a severely disabled child. They saw how the experience would make them better ambassadors for God. What vision will guide you forward from this place, however dark it may seem at the moment, into a life made radiant by your deepest beliefs about what God desires for you?

Take a moment now, and use words to paint a picture of where you will go from here. This picture should capture your vision for where you are headed. When you lose your sense of direction, this picture will steer you back on track. So describe in detail your destination and your next step for moving in that direction.

You Have Everything You Need

Use the Power of Your *Thoughts*

What message are your emotions offering you right now as you contemplate whether to return to an old path or forge a new one? Think about what that message suggests about what *not* to choose and how that shapes what you *will* choose.

Use the Power of Your *Words*

Take a moment now to write your vision for the future. What life are you walking toward? Describe it in vivid detail. Within what time frame do you aim to be living this life?

Use the Power of Your *Actions*

Be decisive. Make a decision about whether you will navigate your way back to your previous path or forge a new path altogether.

Use the Power of *Relationships*

If you need to hear yourself think aloud, talk through your decision with a trusted advisor, family member, or friend.

Use the Power of *Prayer*

Lord, I am at a turning point in my life. I have decided to triumph in the face of adversity. I need direction from You. Your Word promises that if I trust in You with all my heart and don't lean on my own understanding, and if I acknowledge You in all my ways, you will direct my paths (Proverbs 3:5–6, NKJV). I am doing those things, and I believe You will guide me in the right direction. Make Your will and Your way known to me, Lord. Help me hear Your voice above all others. Amen.

Triumph Over Trials: Roland's Story

Roland Martin had been sure his life was completely on track. Then, in the space of a few years, everything derailed. Though he'd worked hard to save his marriage, it disintegrated. His career as a journalist followed suit less than a year later. Struggling to land a job, he sought out freelance assignments to make ends meet—and often came up short.

He remembers thinking, *How in the world am I sitting here with all these skills—I can do radio, television, newspaper, Internet. I can write, I can talk—and I seemingly cannot get an opportunity I want or desire?*

Roland says God's response was, *"I understand, but you are in a period where I am putting so much into you for what is coming down the line. If you were so busy and involved, I would not have your undivided attention."*

God certainly had Roland's attention. As money grew scarce between freelance assignments, he struggled to pay his bills. His leased car was on the verge of being repossessed, and he could no longer afford health insurance. "I was struggling to keep it all together," he says.

It all came to a climax in August 2000 while Roland was on a freelance assignment covering the Democratic National Convention in Los Angeles. During lunch, his side began to hurt. He continued to work, largely because if he stopped he might not get paid. "I had to finish this project. I needed the income," he explains. When the pain persisted, he went to an emergency clinic. But pain medications and a full night of rest still didn't help. Finally, in unbearable agony, he called an ambulance from his hotel room. A burst appendix resulted in a five-day stay in the hospital.

Roland finally arrived back in Houston, but things only got worse. "While I was in the hospital in Los Angeles, my vehicle had been repossessed at the airport." And he was soon hit with the medical bills—nearly $100,000 for surgery and five days in the hospital.

Foreclosure proceedings soon began, and financially overwhelmed, he filed for bankruptcy.

"While all this stuff was going on, it was a faith journey," he says. "About a month before the health problem, God had shared the vision with me and told me to put it on the shelf." That vision included a multimedia journalism business with Roland as a commentator, columnist, television and radio host—an African-American voice with a Christian worldview who could not be pigeonholed with political labels. Roland wrote out the vision in detail in July 2000 and put it away. Though the vision seemed only to move further out of reach, somehow he never doubted that God would bring it all about.

But recovery didn't come easily. Soon after his car was repossessed, a freelance check arrived that he desperately needed to deposit, but no friends were available to take him to the bank several miles from home. "I had to walk to the bank," he remembers. "When I got home, my legs were throbbing. I said to God, *'This is so hard.'*" He sensed a response from God in his spirit, *'Didn't I tell you I'd supply all your needs? Do your legs work?'*" It sounds harsh, but Roland says he learned the lesson that you must use everything you have to get out of your ditch. There is no room for complaining because it could be worse. "I couldn't argue with God's question, *'Do your legs work?'* He was right. He supplied what I needed. Maybe it wasn't as convenient as I would have liked, but I made it to the bank that day."

In the midst of his setbacks, the one bright spot was Roland's growing relationship with a young woman named Jackie. They had met five months after his divorce and nine months before his appendix burst, and she walked with him through all the struggles in his professional and financial life. He saved up to buy her a ring—and finally collected enough the day before their wedding in April 2001.

Two months after the wedding, he landed a six-figure job as editor-in-chief of an online news site aimed at African Americans—and his career has skyrocketed ever since.

Today, the multimedia vision God gave him in the summer of 2000 is a reality. Roland's nationally syndicated newspaper column has been running since 2003. His Chicago-based radio show opened doors for him on network television, and he is now a CNN political analyst and has hosted several faith-based specials for the network. He is the daily commentator for the *Tom Joyner Morning Show,* which airs weekday mornings to a syndicated audience of more than seven million listeners a week. His weekly television show airs on cable.

Roland describes the impact of his setbacks like this:

"In one of his speeches, Dr. Martin Luther King Jr. talks about getting a phone call one night after Mrs. King and the kids had gone to sleep. The viciousness of the hatred in the call was stunning—threatening to kill him and his children. He said he sat down at his kitchen table to pray a prayer that was more intense and deep than he'd ever prayed. Up until that point, he had a theoretical understanding of theology. After that situation, he had a personal understanding of theology.

"When my path took such an expected turn, it gave me an intimate and personal understanding of the power of God's Word in my life. I wouldn't be doing what I do now if I had not gone through those trials. When I speak about faith on the air, I have a level of conviction about it. And I speak openly and freely about it. I don't hide who I am. I don't sugarcoat it."[3]

ROLAND'S LESSONS FROM THE DITCH

- *Positive thoughts matter.* Had I been angry, upset, vindictive, or disobedient—for example, taking money I could have taken during my divorce when God told me not to—I don't believe I would be where I am now.

- *Quit asking, "Why did this happen? Why me?"* If you feel sorry for yourself, you'll stay in the ditch longer.

- *You are not destined to be in that ditch forever.* If you believe in Him enough and you are willing to do the work yourself (remember, faith without works is dead!), then you are going to overcome whatever situation you are in. It requires faith. But it also requires patience.

- *You must develop an appreciation for progress, even seemingly small progress.* When we get knocked into the ditch, we want to come running out immediately. But it doesn't work that way. Consider, for example, if you suffer a stroke. You will have to go through the rehabilitation process to recover. Your mind is likely moving just as fast as it was before the stroke, but you might not be able to talk. You grow frustrated when you move one finger, but in the rehabilitation world, you've reached a milestone. One day you move one finger, then two, then three, and then it's the arm, your toes, your foot, your leg. Then suddenly all those parts work together. Finally, you are in position to walk, but your speech is still messed up. What they teach in rehabilitation is that every movement is a milestone, and each moment is progress.

EIGHT

Do You Need to Redefine Yourself?

Gaining a Clearer Picture of Your Authentic Self and Coming to Terms with Your New Identity

M y client Misha was stuck. It had been a year since her divorce was final, and her ex-spouse was still the topic of conversation every time she got together with friends. And at social engagements, particularly receptions and business events where she had to meet new people, she sometimes lied or skirted the subject of her marital status. She was embarrassed by what she saw as her failure. And she was particularly uncomfortable around church folks, who could sometimes be quite inquisitive. She didn't feel like explaining that she was now divorced. She felt defensive, wanting people to know that she hadn't cheated on her spouse or treated

- *Differentiate between your authentic core self and external factors.*

- *Seize the opportunity to redefine yourself.*

- *Let your circumstances stretch you into a bigger person.*

him badly. Her social anxiety centered on her belief that, as she put it, she now had "a black mark" on her record.

Misha's feelings were creating a roadblock to the next phase of her life because, truthfully, she didn't want a next phase. She hadn't asked for this change; it had been thrust upon her, and she was struggling to accept the bitter reality.

MOVING TOWARD A NEW YOU

Whatever the nature of your own setback, you may be wrestling with similar feelings. If you face a health challenge, it can be a struggle to accept the reality of the disability or diagnosis. If your retirement funds took a major hit with a downturn in the economy, it's difficult to come to terms with reality. You wonder, *How can my years of hard work and savings just disappear like that? There must be some way to get it back.*

The truth is, sometimes we have no way to regain what's been lost. No amount of denial on our part will reverse the situation. As we discussed a few chapters ago, it is what it is. The only way to find peace is to accept the things we cannot change and rebuild from this point. Remember Commitment #2: I will not stare at the closed door.

Often, the deepest pain of an unexpected change comes not from the specific loss but from how it rocks your understanding of who you are. If your identity was based largely on something that has now disappeared or changed irrevocably, you'll find it harder to shift your focus to the future. Your biggest challenge is not necessarily accepting your loss but accepting yourself as you are now. To move forward with your sense of self intact, you will have to learn to believe in yourself—without whatever it is you thought you had to have in order to have worth. You will have to distinguish between your loss and the essence of who you really are.

It's important to recognize that two different types of identity shape your sense of self. The first comes from deep inside—the essence of you. Who you are at the core will not change, no matter what happens to you or around you. If you had a sense of humor before your setback, you will likely have some sense of humor after it. If you were an optimistic person before you landed in the ditch, your optimism will inevitably return—and probably already has. Furthermore, nothing can change your identity as a child of God. So no matter what happens, you can know without a doubt that you are valuable. God still loves you. He walks with you. And your life has meaning.

The second type of identity is external—it is the stuff that shapes how the world sees us. During a setback, we typically lose various things. Some of the lost "stuff" may be material: the house, the car, the money. Sometimes what disappears is less tangible: friendships, social prestige, neighborhoods, access. Sometimes we lose our roles—as a spouse, friend, student, or employee.

Even if we'd like to forget that our stuff is missing, we endure constant reminders of what's been lost in transition. The twenty-something making noise in the parking lot of his apartment complex reminds the newly divorced forty-year-old that he no longer lives in an established, quiet, single-family-home neighborhood. The prompt to mark either *Ms.* or *Mrs.* when purchasing a plane ticket online reminds the widow that after twenty years of marriage she now falls into a new category. The loneliness of the unemployed office worker is exacerbated by the urge to walk down the hall to chat with a co-worker about some new development in the industry. And the person experiencing chronic health issues has constant reminders of his new limitations. He can no longer just get up and do what he'd like; he often has to ask for help.

In the days ahead, it's vital that you remember this truth: *what* you are may have changed but *who* you are remains constant. Use the following questions to reflect on both your unchangeable core identity and your old external identity.

What words best describe who you are? (Avoid using words that simply describe what you do, such as your professional work or the roles you play in your personal relationships.)

What "things" (titles, roles, resources) have previously defined your identity?

FOUR STAGES OF IDENTITY SHIFT

I have found in my own life, as well as in my work coaching clients, that fully transitioning to a new identity after an unexpected change generally follows four stages. Being aware of these stages helps you move through them more easily.

Stage 1: Clinging to the Past

Even when a major change brings positive effects—for example, a layoff that gives you the opportunity to pursue the career you really want—it can be difficult to let go of the way you've defined yourself up to this point. During the first year after I shifted careers and began writing and speaking full time, I clung to my title as founder and president of the Burton Agency, the public relations firm I'd run for four years. While it was true I was founder and still technically president, my motive for using those titles was rooted in discomfort with my new identity. In my mind, the old title carried more weight, and I was reluctant to give it up, even though it had nothing to do with the work I was actually doing and the vision I had for my life moving forward.

Our insecurities—fear of the unknown, fear of the future—may prompt us to cling to our past identity in any number of ways:

- Hiding or denying anything has changed
- Insisting you can still do what you did before even if clearly you cannot
- Refusing to let go of things—whether a possession, title, name, house, or relationship—when it's time to move on
- Refusing to engage in steps that will move you forward

You can start the process of letting go of your old identity by giving yourself permission to fully mourn your loss. Acknowledge any lessons you've learned. If necessary, return to chapter 3 and review some of the lessons about the path that brought you to this point. Then, once you've acknowledged and mourned, choose to pick yourself up and move forward. Remember, self-pity is self-sabotage. Or as Alexander Graham Bell is credited with wisely observing: "When one door closes another door opens; but we so often look so long and so regretfully upon the closed door, that we do not see the ones which open for us."

Stage 2: The Awkward Embrace

Even once you've embraced your new identity, you likely won't feel immediately at ease. Maybe you haven't figured out the right words to describe your situation. Perhaps you're still struggling with embarrassment or shame. You may feel frustrated that people around you seem to be acting differently toward you. Even if their reactions aren't negative, the very idea that people now see you differently may be disturbing.

The fact is, your perception of others' behavior and the reality of their reactions may be worlds apart. You are still sensitive at this stage—sometimes even hypersensitive. This is normal. It may take you some time to get used to your new identity—in fact, certain aspects of it may continue to evolve—but eventually you will become more at ease with the new you. And as you nurture your inner resilience, you'll find that the reactions and perceptions that bother you now gradually lose their power.

Stage 3: Settling In

Researchers who study happiness have actually found something they call the "happiness set point."[1] They contend that 50 percent of your happiness is genetic—it's your predisposition. However, 40 percent of your happiness is comprised of things within your control (intentional activities, such as how you think, what you do daily, who you are around, and so on), and just 10 percent is determined by circumstances. That's why a change in circumstances does not necessarily or permanently change your general level of happiness.

While the initial shock and fear of a traumatic event causes a significant decrease in a person's happiness and well-being, over time people generally return to their previous level of happiness.

What does this mean for you as you settle in to a new identity? It means that, while you may believe the current turmoil and upheaval in your life will lead to long-term misery, the more likely scenario is that you will adapt to the change. The longer you walk in your new identity, the more confidence you will gain in your ability to successfully travel a new path. Though it once may have stung deeply to think about the change forced on you, in this stage you'll find that you're beginning to adjust to your new normal.

Stage 4: Embodying the New You

The final stage of your identity shift is characterized by your full confidence as a person who has learned to thrive despite your setbacks. You are at peace with what happened. You've moved on with your life. You've walked onto your new path and you are living fully. Even if you still carry physical signs of your adversity—such as a disability or a scar—you have conquered your challenges, and so these things no longer define your view of yourself.

IDENTITY CHECK

In order to progress through all four stages of your identity shift, you must first consider the external factors that previously shaped your identity and how those have changed or will change because of your new circumstances. Only then can you identify who you want to become as you shape your comeback.

In Misha's case, she had defined herself, at least in part, by the accomplishments of her former husband. So she resisted letting go of her place in his world, where she'd found validation. She finally admitted that she'd kept her married name, even though she had no children, simply because it tied her to him.

The divorce drastically shook up her sense of self for another reason as well: she'd always been rather judgmental toward people whose marriages ended in divorce, convinced that couples who worked hard enough could save the relationship. And yet here she was. She'd done everything she could to save her marriage, and it still ended.

Her lingering question was, "What does that say about me?"

I asked Misha a healthier question: "What does that say about the belief you previously held?"

She pondered to consider. "I guess my situation doesn't have to condemn me, but maybe I learned a harsh lesson about judgment. You never know what another person's circumstances are. And I think in the past I definitely have rushed to judgment. Now I look at my own circumstances, and I know I did right by my spouse. I went to all the counseling and I'm not saying I was perfect, but God knows I gave it everything I had."

I probed just a little deeper. "What is the new belief that can accurately replace your old belief?"

Her answer reflected a major shift in her thinking: "You know what? My new belief is to not have an opinion about other people's marriages or any of their business, because I have no idea what they are dealing with. My new belief is that if someone else has gone through something as traumatic as I have, I will pray for them. I will listen. I will not judge."

"And what if someone else judges you because you've been through a divorce?" I asked. "How does this new belief help you handle that?"

This question seemed to really hit home, but when she finished mulling it over, she was clear. "I really can't worry about what other people think!" she said emphatically. "There is nothing I can do about other people being judgmental, but pray for them. I'm not saying it won't bother me at all, but I won't let it control my actions and emotions."

"So the two things you've struggled most to accept about life after your divorce are your identity as a married person, particularly as the person married to *him,* and your concern about what it says about you that you are divorced," I pointed out. "You've just had a major shift about the latter, but let's talk about your identity."

She hesitated but was ready to face reality. "I'm scared. I devoted ten years to him. Many of my friends and contacts are because of him," she explained.

"But he's no longer your spouse," I gently reminded her. After a pause, I asked, "What potential do you want to unleash in the next phase of your life?"

"Wow," she said after a long pause. "I've been so focused on the potential I lost that I haven't considered the potential I now have. In fact, I haven't thought about my potential for the future. It's as though I've been thinking my life was over or permanently stuck here in this place."

At this point Misha truly realized the need to redefine herself. To move forward with her life, she'd have to be able to envision her potential beyond the ditch. The starting point was realizing there was life after the death of her marriage. Full acceptance of a new identity wouldn't happen overnight, but it could happen—if she would stop staring at the closed door and begin facing forward.

Resilient People Know . . .

You need balance in how you perceive yourself. Pessimists give others all the credit for the good things that happen and blame themselves entirely for the bad things.

LEARNING TO LOVE THE NEW YOU

A setback is like involuntarily pushing the Reset button on your life. Many of the things that defined you externally may be gone—the job, money, home, city or state, even physical abilities. Yet the pull of your past identity continually attempts to dictate your view of your future self. If you are not careful, the past will be your only reference point, which will limit your ability to fully embrace the remarkable opportunity your setback offers: the opportunity to completely redefine yourself.

When people and things are stripped away, you are left with a clearer picture of your authentic self. What defines you? What truly matters to you? Before you add anything back into your life, you'll want to decide if it truly reflects the identity you want for yourself.

Like Misha, as you seek to understand your new place in the world, you'll find yourself mulling over some difficult questions, including...

Who am I now?
 How will others see me?
Who can I count on?
 What is my value?
Will I be rejected?
 Will I be loved for who I am without the stuff I had
  before my setback?
Do I accept myself in my new reality?

These are not easy questions to wrestle with. The feelings involved in redefining yourself after a major setback can be complex. The way you view yourself and relate to others may have changed. And depending on the specifics of your new reality, it is possible that those close to you no longer see you in the same way; perhaps even their behavior toward you has changed.

Some people may be uncomfortable with your current circumstances—and may even reject you. As painful as that experience is, it can also be liberating. Adversity gives you the chance to discover which people in your life can be depended on to stick with you. Though the loss of any relationship is unfortunate, their decision frees you to enjoy truly authentic relationships with those who love you for who you are at your core, not what you do or what you do for them. Receiving that unconditional love from others is what you need at this time in your life.

More important, though, is your need to show unconditional love to yourself. How?

First of all, don't wallow in regret over what's past. Instead, lift yourself up by words and actions that move you forward. It may evoke a great deal of pain to realize that you have little control over the need to leave behind your old identity. Your divorce may not have been what you wanted. A debilitating accident or health problem was not your doing. A layoff or financial loss may have resulted from others' choices, not yours. And yet, it is what it is. As we've seen, power and peace come from focusing on what you *can* change. What in your situation can you change? Focus on that—and stop dwelling on unproductive thoughts.

Keep in the forefront of your mind the conviction that what happens to you does not define who you are. Bad things happen to wonderful people. The fact that you have been thrown into a ditch does not reflect poorly on your character. Rather, it is a reflection that you are a human being and that life is not always a smooth ride.

Say it out loud if you need to: "What I go through does not define who I am. *How* I go through it defines who I am." Remember that love casts out fear (1 John 4:18, NKJV). When you choose to be loving toward yourself, you will begin to feel yourself cradled in God's strong hand, keeping you safe despite life's hard knocks.

Next, make a decision to allow your identity to shift. This is a huge decision and an absolutely vital aspect of showing yourself unconditional love. You have a choice right now: you can face life with courage and the faith to believe that our God is big enough to carry you through this trial—or you can remain in denial about your reality.

Who do you want to give yourself permission to be that you weren't before?

How do you describe your new identity?

What, specifically, will you have to let go of in order to embrace your new identity?

When my marriage ended, I feared my career would falter because people would judge me for having gone through a divorce. I began to shrink away from opportunities to minister at women's conferences, as though I had something to hide. During a session with my counselor one afternoon, I shared my anxiety. And as I said it out loud, I realized how wrong my perspective was. While I would not have chosen to go through such a painful event, the experience had deepened my faith and strengthened my character. If I chose to swallow my pride and be transparent, what the enemy meant for evil, God would use for good. Many of the women at those women's conferences had been through something just as devastating—or worse—in their own lives. God could use my experience and get the glory for bringing me through—if I didn't shrink from my new identity.

What have you lost that leaves you feeling less valuable than before?

What will it take for you to believe in you without it?

You are still you despite the loss you've endured. You are still valuable. You are still capable of living and loving. You can still make decisions that will shape your future. Today I am asking you to make a decision to let go of the things that used to define you. It will be uncomfortable. It may make you cry. It may make you angry. But the sooner you accept where you are—and who you are—the sooner the truth will set you free.

If you are struggling to accept the truth, pray this prayer:

Lord, Your Word says in John 8:32, "Then you will know the truth, and the truth will set you free." Give me the courage to accept the truth and the hope to believe good things are coming my way despite the bad things I've had to contend with. I trust You that all things work together for good for those of us who love You and are called according to Your purpose (Romans 8:28). Amen.

I believe that years from now you will look back and recognize this moment—this decision to let go of your old life and embrace a new identity—as a pivotal point in your comeback. If you choose now to move forward with courage, I believe you will love the person you've become when you emerge on the other side.

LOOK FOR GROWTH OPPORTUNITIES HIDDEN IN YOUR LOSS

Choosing resilience as a key characteristic of your new identity doesn't negate the depth of your loss; it simply empowers you to acknowledge and pursue the opportunities a setback can offer.

The transformation taking place can expand who you are in ways that you may never have imagined. While the enemy wants you to believe that your security was in the stuff, the abilities, the resources, and the roles you thought identified you, the truth is that your core identity is in God. He created you. He knew the character strengths you would need to triumph in the face of adversity. And now you have the opportunity to put those strengths to work as never before.

Another of the significant opportunities that accompanies loss or setbacks is spiritual growth. Adversity is the point at which our faith can be truly tested. You don't have much opportunity to exercise your faith when things go exactly as you planned. But when the thing you most want or need is largely beyond your control, faith is your only viable option. Passages like Psalm 62:7–8 take on a new significance in the context of a significant setback.

> *My salvation and my honor depend on God;*
> *he is my mighty rock, my refuge.*
> *Trust in him at all times, you people;*
> *pour out your hearts to him,*
> *for God is our refuge.*

Certainly, faith should always be our first resort and we should "trust in him at all times," but when we're honest, we admit that's not always the case. So consider your situation an opportunity to grow deeper in your faith.

As you exercise your faith with perseverance, you have the opportunity to serve as an ambassador for God, inspiring others with your courageous approach to life. You may not be aware that others are observing your attitude and actions; you're simply clinging to God and trusting Him to carry you through. But others—perhaps your children, a neighbor, or a co-worker—are watching how you deal with this challenging time. If you are able to face disappointment and distress yet still praise God, still love others, and still have hope, imagine the impact your faith could have on those God wants to draw closer to Him.

A setback can offer other opportunities for growth too. Maybe there was something you always wanted to try or do, but before your setback, it wasn't feasible. Now, certain priorities and responsibilities have evaporated, freeing you to get much-needed rest and set aside time for reflection. As elements of your life are pruned away, space opens up for new things—ideas and dreams that may have been buried beneath the surface.

Don't fall into the trap of comparing your new opportunities with your old opportunities. Instead, focus on the benefits of your emerging identity. Maybe it paves the way for you to address long-neglected needs and wants, or it brings you joy in ways that were missing before. Your new identity will likely stretch you in unexpected ways. Over time, you may find that your character has developed more depth and your personal passions are finally flourishing.

What growth opportunity is being offered to you right now? Take your time with this one—ponder the question for a moment before you write your answer.

How has your change in circumstances changed where you invest your time and energy?

Where has space opened up in your life, and how would you like to fill it?

Remember, as you navigate your unexpected setback, you can choose to exercise faith on a higher level than you ever have before. You can choose to recognize and pursue the opportunities hidden within your challenge. You can choose growth as you realize that you can handle far more than you ever realized you could. In doing so, you glorify God. You show the power of His Word and His strength working in you to face even the most difficult of circumstances.

As God works through your setback, as you accomplish His purposes, your view of yourself will fundamentally change: you will recognize your ultimate identity as one who is more than a conqueror through Him who loves us (Romans 8:37).

You Have Everything You Need

Use the Power of Your *Thoughts*

Proverbs 23:7 reminds us, "As he thinks in his heart, so *is* he" (NKJV), while Proverbs 29:18 cautions, "Where there is no vision, the people perish" (KJV). Use your thoughts to create a vision for your new identity.

Use the Power of Your *Words*

Put pen to paper and honestly answer each of the questions posed on the previous two pages, if you haven't already done so.

Use the Power of Your *Actions*

Identify the way(s) in which you are clinging to the past or still staring at the closed door. What is one specific action that would indicate you are embracing your new identity? Take that action now, or set a time line and deadline. Ask someone to hold you accountable.

Use the Power of *Relationships*

Now is the time to be clear about who accepts you for who you are rather than what you do. Are there any relationships you need to step back from because they require you to remain in an identity that is no longer your reality?

Use the Power of *Prayer*

Lord, I acknowledge that You are at the center of my identity. You created me. You knew me even before I was formed in my mother's womb (Jeremiah 1:5). Help me to let go of the stuff I thought defined me so I can take hold of the reality that lies before me and walk into a new identity. Help me let go of the past and embrace the present and future. Make it so that my best is yet to come. Amen.

Triumph Over Trials: Quincey's Story

Sometimes a setback is about the tough choices you must make in order to step into your destiny—and about the conflict that ensues when God calls you out of your comfort zone and into your purpose. This was the case for Taft Quincey Heatley. At age twenty-two, with a newly minted degree in mathematics, he landed a job on Wall Street working as an analyst for one of the largest and oldest investment banks in the world. It was a dream come true for Quincey, who describes his philosophy of life at the time as "get wealth, be happy."

"As a child, it seemed the most successful people had money," he says. "I always heard my dad complain about money. I wanted to tell my children no because they shouldn't have something, not because I didn't have enough money." He would later learn that his dad's "complaints" were more about frugality than lack, but his mind was made up. He wanted success, and success meant money.

"Growing up black in a small southern town, I wanted to break the myths and stereotypes of us as poor," he explains. "I was maintaining this image—a sharp-dressed, African-American male who had it together. Having it together meant financial security and material possessions, but the truth is, I didn't have peace." Still, he persisted in keeping up the image. He recalls walking into the Ferragamo store in Manhattan and buying the most expensive pair of shoes—with a price tag of eight hundred dollars—just because he could. Then he headed to Barneys and spent more than three thousand dollars on two suits, two shirts, and two ties. "From an ego-stroking standpoint, it was great, but it was so fleeting."

By age twenty-five, he'd been promoted to senior analyst and was earning six figures with very few expenses. He and his roommate split the bill for their two-thousand-dollars-a-month brownstone, and he had no student loans, no car loan, no consumer debt. The hours were grueling—he worked past eight o'clock most nights, but the car service home and the expensed meals eased the pain of long hours. And the financial payoff was remarkable. If he could continue up the ladder, his next promotion would *double* his income. He earned the highest rating of any analyst in his group, but two years in a row he was passed over for promotion. In fact, in the second instance, someone below him was promoted over him. It felt like a slap in the face.

The disappointment prompted Quincey to take a hard look at his life. "I had put all my worth and value into how others judged me rather than how God saw me," he says. "I was trying to open closed doors, but it was like God was telling me, 'The path you want to take is not the path I have for you.'" Years earlier, while in college, Quincey had sensed God calling him to pastor. But he had also sensed God telling him that an understanding of business would be an important part of his ministry. So his venture onto Wall Street had made sense. But now, after being turned down a second time for promotion, he wondered, *Is this a sign?*

"I couldn't stand the idea that I had to work with the guy who was promoted over me," he says. The company gave him the option to stay in his position for another year, but he decided to quit. "I admit a lot of it was pride. I was like, I don't *need* this job." He'd saved enough money to last almost a year without working. So he decided to apply to seminary. He had planned all along to make the transition, but it was happening sooner than he thought it would.

He prayed about where to apply, and the only school he felt led to in his spirit was Princeton Theological Seminary. He considered other programs where he could get a dual degree—a master's in theology and an MBA. But he did so poorly on the entrance exam for business school that he gave up on that idea. "Princeton was the only school I considered that didn't have a graduate program in business. It was like a confirmation of God's plan for me." But the plan didn't work out the way Quincey intended.

"I needed a recommendation from my pastor as a part of my application," he recalls. "I had begun the ordination process through my church a couple of years earlier, but the process was not complete. My pastor informed me he could not write my recommendation until I went before the board of deacons and preached my trial sermon." That wouldn't happen until the following June, and by then it would be too late to apply to seminary. "So now, I've quit my job and I can't go to seminary for another year after I'd planned to! It was so humbling. I was completely blindsided."

Quincey was running through his money faster than he'd anticipated. "Even though I had no money coming in, I continued to spend as though I had a job, trying to keep up this lifestyle," he admits. "It was all I knew since graduating college. I was going out, buying stuff I didn't need. I was in denial. By March, I was completely out of money." He took a part-time job at his church, working in an after-school program for a little over minimum wage.

He began looking for a stable job in February. "Of course I entertained thoughts I should have kept my investment banking job," he says. "But I couldn't go back there." It took six months to land a job that paid 40 percent less than his previous position. But, he says, "The job covered my needs and helped me get back on track."

With a new job, his trial sermon preached, and the ordination in hand, he applied to seminary. He was accepted to Princeton, the only school he applied to, and began the three-year program in the fall of 2004.

"My biggest struggle was not being able to live the lifestyle I coveted," he says. "I was wrestling with becoming this new person, but I also had to come to terms with how others viewed me now that I was so serious about my relationship with God." His struggle continued when he left his new job to head back to school. "As a grad student, I took out loans for school, didn't have a job, moved into a dorm room, used a community shower, and ate in the cafeteria. It wasn't the end of the world, but it was a stark contrast to my brownstone and my life in New York."

He says his new approach to life was, "God, are you pleased with this?" instead of, "Quincey, are you pleased with this?" Stripped of money, a fancy lifestyle, and the perceived admiration of others, he came to know God in a whole new way. "I got the revelation that *God is my source*," he says. "He had to take me out of my environment for me to really get it. During my three years in school, He provided for me in ways I'd never seen before."

After graduate school, he accepted an invitation from Dr. Cynthia Hale, senior pastor at Ray of Hope Christian Church in Atlanta, Georgia, to serve as the church's executive pastor. Quincey is now living in his purpose. What he gave up financially to follow his calling pales in comparison to what he's gained spiritually. "I was out of place," he says. "I was following a career path that was not my calling and purpose. God allowed me to experience corporate America so that I could see that wasn't it. *He* is it."[2]

Quincey's Lessons from the Ditch

- *Seize the opportunity to reevaluate.* Look at the path you were on when the setback happened and ask, Was that the right path for me anyway?

- *Know there is a purpose at work.* Sometimes the setback happens to get you off the path. Sometimes the setback happens to strengthen you for the journey.
- *Always, always remain humble.* Humility was the key that I had to learn. My life is not about me. It is about God and fulfilling His purpose for my life. God is the goal.
- *God is your source.* He will keep you throughout your journey. He will be merciful and gracious.

NINE

What's the Best Way to Get There from Here?

*Designing Your Comeback,
Step by Step*

Remember Claire, the accomplished sales executive who lost her mother, two jobs, her life savings, and a marriage all in the span of a year? Today, three years later, Claire is vice president of development for a major media organization. She is rebuilding financially, emotionally, and spiritually—one step at a time.

This resilient woman has nurtured an attitude that declares, "I made it before. I can make it again." Claire designed a comeback using her strengths, and she's following her plan while remaining open to God's adjustments along the way.

Now it's your turn to design your own comeback plan. A plan gives you a road map

- Seek God's direction for your next steps.

- Map out a destination, direction, and daily actions.

- Persevere with patience and determination.

to navigate your way to your destination. The word picture you painted at the end of chapter 7—the detailed description of your vision—is the starting point for your plans, along with the identity you defined in chapter 8.

KEYS TO WISE PLANNING

Before you begin mapping out your first steps, let's take a look at what God says about planning in the book of Proverbs:

> Commit to the LORD whatever you do, and he will establish your plans. (16:3)

> Plans fail for lack of counsel, but with many advisers they succeed. (15:22)

> In their hearts humans plan their course, but the LORD establishes their steps. (16:9)

I believe these verses offer three key pieces of wisdom as you prepare to step out on your path toward a better destination:

1. Put God First. If You Are Within His Will, Success Will Come

As much as we would like to believe it, no amount of planning will trump God's will. As you plan, be prayerful. Surrender your will to God's will. The journey may not be as smooth as you would like, and you may encounter more bumps along the way. Things may not come together as quickly as you envision, and the process of recovery may present the biggest test of faith you've ever encountered—possibly more challenging than the circumstance that knocked you off course. Will you pass the test? Absolutely—if you put God first, if you submit fully to His molding and shaping process. Your faith will expand. Your perseverance will deepen. Your understanding of who God is will increase in ways that would not have been possible without this experience.

So as you lay out your plan, commit first and foremost to serving and glorifying God. If you do, you'll be prepared to watch for God's presence at every turn, even those that seem to take you backward. In fact, pause for a moment and write your own prayer of commitment right now.

2. Seek Wise Counsel and Advisors

Your plans have a greater chance of success if you reach out to others. Though you may feel alone in your circumstances, many are traveling— or have previously traveled—a similar road. And many others have information about how to navigate your path. Don't go it alone.

Remember one of Faith Proietti's lessons from the ditch: "Learn as much as you can so you can make good and healthy choices. Learn as much as possible about your disease, divorce proceedings, what is needed to survive in your career industry—whatever touches your present challenge." Here's what the Bible says about the value of looking beyond yourself for insight:

Get wisdom. Though it cost all you have, get understanding.
(Proverbs 4:7)

> Wisdom is found in those who take advice. (Proverbs 13:10)

> For lack of guidance a nation falls, but victory is won through many advisers. (Proverbs 11:14)

Of course, counselors and advisors include not only others who have been through similar challenges, but also those whose specialized knowledge can help you chart the best course of action. Depending on your setback, such individuals can include lawyers, financial advisors, health-care providers, mentors, role models, career coaches, therapists, and marriage counselors. Some of the people you identified as potential resources in chapter 6 could also be counted among your team of advisors.

In what specific areas would you most benefit from counsel?

Who is the person best suited to assist you in each of these areas?

3. Be Flexible

As you design your own personal plan, you'll want to be fully committed to it but not dependent on it. In other words, don't base your definition of success on checking off every box on your list, but on knowing that you are walking God's perfect path for you—even if it means taking an alternate route instead of the one you've planned. Resilient people expect change to be a part of life.

As we've seen before, serenity comes not only from changing the things we can but also accepting that some things are beyond our power to control. As you lay out your plans today, you cannot anticipate all of the situations or opportunities you'll encounter along your new path. "In their hearts humans plan their course, but the LORD establishes their steps" (Proverbs 16:9). No matter how carefully you chart your course, you cannot see the big picture. But God does. Be persistently prayerful so that you are sensitive to the voice of the Holy Spirit, continually gathering information and direction to help you better understand what your next steps should be.

Much as a ship's captain makes course corrections to navigate around potential problems on the way to a destination, you'll want to remain flexible and open to God's direction and any adjustments He guides you to make along the way.

DESIGNING THE ESSENTIAL ELEMENTS
OF YOUR COMEBACK

To be effective, your comeback plan must be designed to include the three essential *D*s:

1. Destination
Your destination is the vivid and specific goal that ultimately inspires you to persevere. It's the vision you laid out as a word picture in chapter 7. The destination needs to be so clear and compelling that it will propel you forward even when you face roadblocks and bumps in the road. Though you may occasionally stumble, you won't give up because you know a better future is waiting for you.

However, as you forge ahead, resist the temptation to focus too intensely on your destination. Gazing at the future for too long may cause you to miss out on the riches of the present moment or distract you from seeing the immediate next step that will take you forward. Imagine your destination as a mountain that is miles in the distance. If you stare at the mountain your entire journey instead of at the path in front of you, you are bound to miss some turns and trip over obstacles. Instead, you'll want to glance at the mountain occasionally to orient yourself and stir your motivation.

Answer the following questions to help you identify your destination:

Describe in detail the destination you are headed toward. What does it look like? Look back at the description you crafted in chapter 7 and expand on it, if necessary.

What is it about this destination that will inspire you even when you face obstacles in your path?

When do you hope to arrive at your destination?

2. Direction

Based on your destination, you'll identify goals—milestones, so to speak—that lead you in the right direction and let you know whether or not you are on track. Goals are not action steps. Goals are measurable, purposeful objectives that lead to your destination.

For example, if you are currently in Miami, Florida, and you plan to drive to Santa Monica, California, you'll consider the directions you need to reach your destination and then break it up into specific, intermediate goals. You might set a goal of driving up I-95 to Jacksonville. Your next goal is to get onto I-10, which will fortunately take you straight to Santa Monica. Your goal might be to get to New Orleans on the second day, then drive through Houston to Tucson, and then on your last day, arrive in Santa Monica.

The same holds true as you navigate your way along the path to your destination. Each goal will lead you in a specific direction and provide mile markers to measure your progress. This sense of continual progress provides critical momentum for achieving your comeback.

The following questions will help you set your direction:

As you journey toward your destination, what milestones will you aim for? (Identify at least ten.)

What signs will warn you if you're moving in the wrong direction?

Look at your list of milestones. Write each milestone in the form of a goal that is specific, measurable, achievable—and set a deadline.

The process of starting over is not always smooth. Even if you're making progress, you may experience mixed emotions as you reach milestones that are familiar and remind you of life prior to your setback. The sense of repeating the past can be a frustrating reminder of all you've lost. Later we'll discuss how to joyfully celebrate those familiar milestones anyway. But first, let's look at the third component in designing your comeback.

3. Daily Actions

Your ability to move from setback to comeback will be directly related to the intensity with which you focus on consistent action. Ecclesiastes 5:3 says, "For the dream comes through much effort and the voice of a fool through many words" (NASB). Your comeback plan isn't just something to talk about in general terms; it needs to include daily actions—specific steps you will take to move toward your destination. These deliberate daily actions lead, one by one, directly toward your intermediate goals. Identify daily actions that are manageable so you can have the satisfaction of actually accomplishing them. Each small success will motivate you to continue taking more steps toward your larger goals.

Earlier I mentioned the concept of self-efficacy—believing that you can achieve what you set out to do. You build self-efficacy by achieving small successes that nurture your confidence to attempt bigger goals.

After a setback, you are vulnerable to self-doubt and a lack of confidence. Generating "wins" counters that vulnerability. Remember, baby steps taken consistently and in the right direction will lead you to your destination.

The following questions will help you determine your daily actions.

Choose the goal that is most important to you. What are the bite-sized action steps that will lead to this goal? By bite-sized, I mean action steps that can be accomplished in a day. (The most effective way to reach your goals is to concentrate on them one at a time. So choose one goal to focus on, then once that is attained, focus on the next.)

What potential distractions or obstacles might prevent you from taking each action step toward this goal?

What could you do to eliminate or minimize each distraction?

Are there any actions for which you can partner with someone who will help? If so, who can help you take action consistently?

PROGRESS IS A PROCESS

In coaching my clients toward their authentic path, I've learned that achieving success is rarely a smooth and predictable process; rather, it requires continual evaluation and recalculation—in other words, learning and action. Obviously, this is why resilience is such a key indicator of ultimate success!

> ### Resilient People Know...
>
> Practicing patience in the small things prepares you to be patient in the big things. Research shows that grit—your ability to persevere in the face of obstacles—is directly related to your ability to be patient and delay gratification.

I help clients see the big picture so they can develop an overall vision—or destination—for where they are headed. Then, just as you're doing, we develop a course of action to help the client achieve his or her intermediate goals and move in the right direction. By the end of each session, the client identifies and commits to specific next steps for achieving those goals. At the start of our subsequent session, I inevitably pose three questions:

1. What did you learn as a result of taking action based on the next steps you committed to in our previous session?

2. What obstacles and opportunities lie before you as you continue to forge ahead toward the vision? How can you navigate through or around the obstacles? How can you make the most of the opportunities?

3. Based on the new information (lessons learned from taking action and from naming obstacles and opportunities that lie ahead), what steps will you take before our next session?

You can use this same set of questions as you forge ahead. This is called self-coaching, and you can accomplish it in a couple of different ways.

First, you can journal your answers, a method that is extremely effective, especially if you allow yourself the time and space to fully answer the questions. Be sure to notice the thoughts and feelings that each question provokes and then spend some time reflecting on them. Commit yourself to being flexible. Give yourself permission to follow a few rabbit trails as you explore your thoughts and observe your feelings. Above all, be honest. God often shows up when you take the time to be self-reflective, to still yourself long enough for the truth to surface. It isn't necessarily that you have been lying to yourself. It's just that, in the midst of chaos, fear, and confusion, the truth often gets buried. Our real thoughts and emotions—the internal stuff that reveals our authentic self—get smothered by all of the external stimuli battling for attention. When you invite God to shine a searchlight in your heart, you'll begin to peel back the layers and unearth the answers you're looking for.

Another helpful advantage of journaling as a self-coaching method is that it creates a record that you can refer to in the future. As we move forward and get caught up in new circumstances, it's easy to forget what we have already discovered. Self-coaching through journaling provides the opportunity to remind yourself of what you already know. It also enables you to see the progress you've made over time.

Some people have breakthroughs more easily by talking things out rather than writing them out, so another way to coach yourself is to get a friend to help you. Give this person the three questions I just listed and ask him or her to pose the questions to you without inserting personal opinions or insights. Instead, your friend is to act as a facilitator—a collaborator in your growth and learning. This person's presence can make it easier for you to answer your questions honestly and objectively.

Here are a few more tips for engaging with the person who is acting as your coach:

- Ask your friend to pose open-ended questions, while avoiding *yes-no* and *why* questions, which can leave you defensive. Use *what, how, when,* and so on.

- Request that she give you time and space to think without feeling pressured to quickly come up with the answer. Uninterrupted silence provides time for you to think and to reflect.

- Invite him to ask additional questions based on what he hears (or doesn't hear). Sometimes what you don't say is just as telling as what you do.

- Ask that she resist the urge to give you the answer. Sometimes the person asking the questions feels she has your answer. But it is critical that she allows you to think things through. You are more likely to move forward when you own your answers rather than having them handed to you.

- Ask your friend to be sure to ask you two questions before you close your time together. First, a question that inspires action (for example, So what action do you want to take and by when? or What will you do differently in the future?). Second, a question that gives you a chance to reflect on what was most valuable about the conversation (for example, What do you most need to remember from this conversation? or What was most helpful about talking this through?).

Practice Patience

As you navigate your way, the process of learning and action will require patience. You may feel anxious to get your life back to where you want it, to recapture your normal routine. But the truth is, this *is* your new normal. Being in process is just a natural part of this season in your life. Can you embrace that for the time being? Will you ask God for the grace to simply rest in the process rather than fighting against it? If you can get comfortable with not always knowing the answers, you will find contentment even while your goals are yet out of reach.

When you reach a point where you don't feel certain about your next action step, trust that God is at work, and in His timing He'll reveal what to do next. In the past I would often think that I was ready for something and then set out to make it happen—only to discover that I needed to experience some growth and learning before I took that next step. At other times, I needed to wait for the right circumstances to line up in order for the vision to be fully realized.

When you wait on God and trust Him to provide the answers, when you surrender yourself to divine timing and heed the voice of the Holy Spirit, you position yourself for greater rewards than you may previously have imagined. Ephesians 3:20 describes God as "him who is able to do immeasurably more than all we ask or imagine."

Whenever you feel a lack of clarity, consider these coaching strategies:

Try waiting as an action step. People regularly say, "God answered my prayer," meaning they got what they asked for. But God doesn't just answer prayer with a "Yes." Sometimes He says, "No." Often, He says, "Wait."

All three are legitimate answers. It may sound counterintuitive, but waiting is an action step. In my work as an executive coach, I often have occasion to ask clients to do nothing as a next step. And at the next session, they almost invariably share amazing lessons they've learned from that. You too may find that God moves in incredible ways when you trust Him enough to be still.

Take a small step, then notice what happens. If you're feeling torn about what direction to take, sometimes the best thing you can do is begin to move slightly in one direction. Notice what happens when you do. Do you feel at peace? Are doors opening easily, or do you seem to be struggling with no purposeful outcome? Sometimes taking a small step provides clarity about whether or not to continue on a particular path.

Delve into an area of life you've been neglecting. Often we're held back in one area because we're focused on other matters. Until those are addressed and resolved, your answer will not come. For example, my client Diana had a very successful consulting company and came to me for help as she focused on propelling the company to the next level. She wanted to expand to three new cities over the next few years. After several sessions, though, I noticed she often jokingly referenced her nearly nonexistent social life. She'd spent the previous eight years growing a successful business, and now that she was approaching age forty, she wanted someone to share it with. She was wistful as she talked about how quickly the years had gone by and how she didn't want to be in the same place at age fifty. It was painful for her to realize that much of her success had come at the expense of a personal life. But it also reinforced her determination to reclaim her schedule. Through coaching, she discovered that she needed to carve out some breathing room to simply enjoy life.

What have you been avoiding? Consider your waiting period an opportunity to address a neglected area that needs your attention, such as nurturing a relationship, taking care of yourself, going back to school, taking control of your finances, or getting your career on track. You know what it is for you.

Connect with God by talking—and then listening. James 4:8 says, "Come near to God and he will come near to you." As you contemplate a next step, make sure your decisions are rooted firmly in the divine guidance that is available to you when you become still and quiet and listen.

Navigate Around the Obstacles

Planning your course of action also means preparing for the obstacles that you are bound to encounter. Coping with obstacles takes determination— the type of determination epitomized by a group of friends trying to help their paralyzed friend in the New Testament:

> Some men came carrying a paralyzed man on a mat and tried to take him into the house to lay him before Jesus. When they could not find a way to do this because of the crowd, they went up on the roof and lowered him on his mat through the tiles into the middle of the crowd, right in front of Jesus. When Jesus saw their faith, he said, "Friend, your sins are forgiven."…
>
> He said to the paralyzed man, "I tell you, get up, take your mat and go home." Immediately he stood up in front of them, took what he had been lying on and went home praising God. (Luke 5:18–20, 24–25)

These men didn't allow the crowds surrounding the house to block their path to success. They knew their answer was inside, and they were determined to find a way in, even though gaining access would not be quick and easy.

In our fast-paced culture, could it be that we have become so used to getting what we want quickly and easily that we've failed to value the virtues of determination, patience, and perseverance? Authentic confidence says, "I may not know how to get it right now, but there is a way, and I am determined to find it." You may have to work harder than you thought. You may have to be creative. You may have to step outside your comfort zone and do it differently from the way everyone around you does.

But when it comes to recovering from your setback, success will inevitably mean finding a way to deal with obstacles. In fact, the obstacles often are ideally designed to help you develop the character traits you need to succeed in the next phase of your life.

Focus on the following four keys when you come up against something that hinders your progress toward your destination:

1. Make a decision to find a way. Determination begins with a decision to succeed, whatever it takes. The people in Luke 5 wanted healing for their friend, and they made a decision to do whatever it took to get it. Get clear about what you are aiming for, commit to it fully, and refuse to allow distractions to steal your focus. Keep your destination, direction, and daily actions in front of you. Each day ask yourself, *What is my focus for today?*

2. Manage your expectations. Don't expect a fast and easy recovery. It is possible that your answers may come quickly and easily, but don't count on it. More often than not, recovery comes when you persevere over time. Be prepared for the long haul. In the next chapter we'll talk more about how to manage your thoughts in ways that help you carry on with confidence, even when progress is slower than you'd like.

3. Stop focusing on the obstacle and start looking for the opportunity. The men with the paralyzed friend weren't focused on the crowds blocking access to the house. They didn't try to push their way through. They realized that their real problem was not the crowd. The real problem was that their friend needed to be healed and a miracle worker was inside, if they could just get to Him. Seeing that the traditional way of gaining access to the house would not work, they focused on finding another way. When you run up against an obstacle to achieving your goal, stop and consider your alternatives. Write them all down. If you have trouble identifying options, brainstorm with a wise and trusted friend. Research your possible choices. Pray and listen for alternative paths that would still lead to your destination.

4. Do what you have to do. Anything truly worth having is worth working for. Be willing to do whatever is necessary to push on toward your destination—including being willing to fail. Complaining won't change things. Feeling sorry for yourself won't either. Dig your heels in and be determined! Blaze a trail if necessary. On the other side of your obstacle, your reward awaits you. Ask yourself, *What character trait is God trying to help me develop as I work around this obstacle?*

You don't need an elaborate plan to succeed, but you do need some kind of plan—a series of actions that will lead you to your vision. Along the way, as circumstances unfold, you may need to make adjustments. As God prompts you and as you see needed changes, reshape your plan. Allow your vision to be your compass, pointing you in the right direction when you get off track.

Most important, don't overwhelm yourself with *too many plans.* Keep the actions simple and doable. Measure your progress in small increments. Celebrate as you reach each milestone. Acknowledge how far you've come. Maintaining positive thoughts about your progress and your plan is critical. In fact, we'll delve into a plan for managing your thoughts in the next chapter.

You Have Everything You Need

Use the Power of Your *Thoughts*

Refer back to the coaching questions in this chapter to think through your best course of action to move toward your new destination.

Use the Power of Your *Words*

It's not enough to simply think through your plan. Write it out in concrete detail. Take time now while the thoughts and ideas are still fresh in your mind.

Use the Power of Your *Actions*

Do not procrastinate. Set a date by which you will take your first step forward.

Use the Power of *Relationships*

Share your plan and time line with someone who believes in you and can serve as an accountability partner. Give that person permission to check in with you. If possible, schedule regular time together to discuss the learning that is taking place as you forge ahead.

Use the Power of *Prayer*

Lord, I want my plan to be aligned with Your plan. And I want the boldness to forge ahead without hesitation. Help me to be flexible enough to make course corrections as I gain new knowledge and understanding. And help me work through the inevitable obstacles I will face as I take steps forward. Help me to stay encouraged. Remind me to notice my thinking so that doubts and frustrations do not cause me to be counterproductive. Instead, anoint me with the grace to handle anything the enemy throws my way! Amen.

TEN

Are Your Thoughts Holding You Back?

*Thinking Carefully
About How You Think*

V eronica was a stay-at-home mom with three children when her husband, Russ, lost his job as a construction foreman. He received a small severance package that kept them afloat for about three months, but with little savings and no job interviews, the financial pressure soon grew intense. Then a car accident in which Russ was at fault left him with a back injury. Not only was he out of work, but he was also physically unable to do the work for which he was most qualified: construction.

Out of work and physically out of commission, Russ could have spiraled downward into depression. But he didn't. "I don't know how, but I believe God will cover us," Russ

- *Pay attention to what you say to yourself about your circumstances.*

- *Identify and replace counterproductive thoughts.*

- *Develop a habit of optimism.*

told himself every day. He reached out to friends and family. He talked to his two brothers to get advice about his options and brainstorm for ideas and contacts. Like manna from heaven, perfectly timed blessings and financial opportunities made it possible for them to put food on the table and keep the bills paid. One month, it was a tax refund. Another month, a friend from Veronica's pre-mommy job called and invited her to do a temp project.

Russ was resilient. He maintained a positive attitude. He persevered in his job search, and he believed the right position would come at the right time.

Veronica, on the other hand, was a bundle of nerves. In fact, her anxiety affected her interactions with Russ and the children. She was irritable and impatient. Having grown up poor, she believed her worst fear was about to come true: they would lose their house and be out on the street, and she would no longer be able stay home with the kids. Although none of these worries was realized, she became depressed nevertheless. Veronica's thoughts spiraled out of control daily as she imagined worst-case scenarios of what might yet happen to their family.

During his sixth month of unemployment, Russ finally landed a job at his brother's company—with better benefits than he'd had before. When their circumstances changed, Veronica's anxiety eased at last. But wouldn't it have been so much better if she had been able to go through the setback with a sense of peace? Worry and anxiety didn't make the recovery happen any more quickly.

Literally everything we do, say, or feel begins with a thought. Sometimes our thoughts occur so rapidly or are so automatic that we don't even notice them. Still, they directly influence our actions and reactions. That's why one of the most important strategies for building resilience is to be aware of *what* you are thinking *while* you are thinking it.

When you face adversity, your thoughts can either lead you to a brighter outlook or lure you to a dark, lonely, and frustrated place. They can lift you out of the ditch or dig a new one in which to bury your dreams.

The enemy wants to use your setback to destroy your dreams, your trust in God, your hopes for the future—and turning your own thoughts against you is a favorite tactic of his. This is spiritual warfare, so you don't want to enter the battle ill equipped.

> The weapons we fight with are not the weapons of the world. On the contrary, they have divine power to demolish strongholds. We demolish arguments and every pretension that sets itself up against the knowledge of God, and we take captive every thought to make it obedient to Christ. (2 Corinthians 10:4–5)

In other words, you want to be so conscious of your thoughts that you are able to take them "captive" and make them obey. Earlier we explored how the choice to conquer your fears is crucial to climbing out of the ditch. But as you pursue your comeback, deliberately thinking about your thinking is absolutely vital. Doing so will enhance your ability to remain focused on your destination, direction, and daily actions. This kind of self-awareness takes practice, but when you get good at it, you will be amazed at how you are able to change your attitude, improve your mood, and maintain a sense of optimism even as you confront inevitable challenges along the way.

MAKING YOUR THOUGHTS OBEY

Dr. Aaron Beck, a psychiatrist born in 1921, revolutionized the practice of psychology in the 1960s with the idea that thoughts create emotions, and emotions are a key factor in predicting who will be resilient and who will crack in the face of adversity. Early in his therapy practice, Dr. Beck noticed that the results of psychoanalysis were not always as effective as he'd like in helping his patients, many of whom suffered from depression and anxiety. Dr. Beck took note of the thoughts these patients shared— thoughts such as *I never do anything right* or *I'm not lovable.* Patients seemed to talk about these thoughts as much as they talked about their emotions, and he made a connection between such thoughts and the emotions that led to depression.

Over time, Beck's observations and research led him to develop a new approach to therapy, based on equipping patients to identify and evaluate their own negative thought patterns, or "cognitions," as he labeled them. This approach—called *cognitive therapy*—is now widely used to help people break free of the distorted thinking that keeps them from moving forward.

Cognitive therapy works for most people because it teaches you how to notice counterproductive thoughts and how to change those thoughts to more accurate, productive ones. In changing your thoughts, you change your emotions and your reactions to the adversities that come your way.

Consider Natalie's story. A series of three bad breakups in five years has left her ready to give up on love altogether. The last breakup was particularly hard on her emotionally because she and her boyfriend had talked about marriage and children and she thought he might really be *the one.* It turns out he wasn't. Natalie no longer feels free to be herself when she meets someone new; her confidence in her own attractive personality has disintegrated. So she remains closed, doesn't reach out much or smile, and rarely socializes with new people.

When the subject of her love life comes up, here are some of Natalie's frequent thoughts:

- *Something must be wrong with me.*
- *Men like women who are not as successful as I am, so I should downplay my career when I meet someone new.*
- *I'm getting older and I'm not as attractive as I used to be.*
- *Maybe it's just a fairy tale that Mr. Right exists.*
- *I'm lousy at this relationship thing and I always will be.*
- *I'm not very good at choosing boyfriends.*

As you can imagine, these thoughts lead to emotions such as fear, sadness, embarrassment, and anxiety about the future. And all of this together could lead to depression.

Major setbacks and unexpected turns often prompt us to question what we thought we knew about ourselves and our lives. We can easily fall into the habit of ruminating on counterproductive thoughts. *Rumination* basically means mulling over the same thought repeatedly, chewing on the same idea rather than moving on. *Counterproductive* refers to any thoughts that undermine your ability to bounce back, move forward, be effective, or lead a fulfilling life.

You can actually think yourself into a depression by meditating on thoughts that weaken and drain you. We know from God's Word, though, that we are to do just the opposite. In fact, just after instructing us to "not be anxious about anything," the Bible says, "Whatever is true, whatever is noble, whatever is right, whatever is pure, whatever is lovely, whatever is admirable—if anything is excellent or praiseworthy—think about such things" (Philippians 4:6, 8).

This is not to say that we should never think about something that is negative; sometimes the truth *is* negative and you need to acknowledge that honestly. We're talking specifically in terms of thoughts that are counterproductive—they weaken you rather than strengthen you. Philippians 4:8 directs us to think about things that are "true" and "right" and "pure." This means you must be careful to notice your negative thoughts and question them by asking, Is that really true? or Is that entirely true? When you identify part or all of a thought as false or inaccurate, you take the counterproductive thought captive and make it obedient by lining it up with truth.

In Natalie's case, her thought about being lousy at relationships might be partly true. Her history of breakups suggests that Natalie really isn't very good at love relationships. In fact, her childhood didn't offer much opportunity for her to learn relationship skills. Her father was married three times and is currently single. Her mother was married for twelve years to Natalie's father, but when the marriage ended, she closed herself off from relationships and focused solely on her children. Her children are now in their thirties, and she has never dealt directly with the pain and betrayal she experienced in her marriage.

So it would be accurate to say Natalie didn't learn how to be in a healthy relationship while growing up, and she hasn't yet mastered that skill as an adult. However, that does not mean Natalie will never be good at a love relationship. To take captive this thought—*I'm lousy at this relationship thing and I always will be*—and make it line up with truth, she has to first admit the part that is true (she hasn't been very effective at building a lasting relationship) and dispute the part that is not true (that because she isn't good now, she never will be in the future). So her new and productive thought is: *My past relationship mistakes do not have to define me. I will learn from them and seek out relationship role models so I can enjoy a loving, lasting relationship in the future.*

By acknowledging what is true, you can take charge and address the problem directly. By disputing what is not true, you take captive the counterproductive part of your thought and reject it. It is no longer something you believe. Then you can replace it with a productive, empowering thought that helps you create a better future.

CHANGE YOUR THOUGHTS, CHANGE YOUR LIFE

Nurturing a conscious awareness of your thought life is a crucial skill for persevering on your journey. Your thoughts will be your constant companions along the way. Repeatedly choosing thoughts that are accurate and empowering will give you the strength to keep going, even in the face of seemingly insurmountable odds.

The following ideas have been adapted from the work of Dr. Andrew Shatté and Dr. Karen Reivich, who acknowledge they based many of their concepts on those of Dr. Aaron Beck, the father of cognitive behavioral therapy.[1] This approach will help you choose thoughts that will propel you forward rather than hold you back. As you put these principles into practice, you will see that they are aligned with the principles of God's Word.

It's All Connected

Building self-awareness of your thought life so that you can adjust your thinking begins with understanding the essential elements of counter-productive thinking:

Trigger ➔ Thoughts ➔ Reactions

Let's look at each of these three elements in detail to see how they work together.

Trigger. A trigger is simply an event, adversity, or challenge that triggers stress or negativity for you. In Natalie's case, a trigger can be going to visit her sister's family, where she is reminded of what it might be like to be married with children, something she eventually wants for herself. If your setback impacted your finances, a trigger could be something routine, such as grocery shopping. Whereas you used to buy everything on your list and maybe toss in a few extras, now you have to calculate how much you are spending before you get to the register. Other things that may serve as triggers include a difficult conversation, doing poorly at something meaningful to you, or even a scene on television that reminds you of pain or disappointment in your own life.

Thoughts. A trigger sends thoughts immediately running through your head. I'm not talking about how you feel here, but what you think. These are thoughts that come to you *in the heat of the moment*—not what you think after you've had time to process the situation. Natalie's thoughts might include, *I'll never have a family* or *My life is so off track* or *I've always been the less attractive sister.* The person at the grocery store who is counting every penny may think, *I'm going to miscalculate what's in the basket and be embarrassed when I have to tell the cashier to put an item back.* Imagine if your thoughts were on display like an electronic billboard in Times Square; how would they read?

Reactions. Your reaction can be one of two things, or both: (1) your emotions or feelings about the situation, and/or (2) the action you take as a result of the thought. Action can be something you do or choose not to do, or something you say or choose not to say. Each reaction, whether an internal feeling or an external response, can be directly linked to a thought. So Natalie's trigger, which caused her to think, *I'll never have a family,* might cause her to react by feeling sad (emotion) and leaving her sister's home earlier than planned (action). The person who becomes stressed at the grocery store and has a thought about miscalculating might then feel anxious (emotion) and preemptively remove a couple of items from his grocery cart (action).

Follow the Trail

Just for a little practice in building the self-awareness that allows you to take your thoughts captive, think back to a recent trigger that led to a counterproductive reaction—hesitation or procrastination, feelings of giving up or helplessness, an argument or heated response. While the sequence of events is Trigger ➋ Thoughts➋ Reactions, it is often easier to identify your thoughts if you pinpoint them last. The reason is that we are usually clear about what happened and clear about how we reacted. However, we are often unaware of the thoughts in the heat of the moment that prompted our reactions. Only by building your awareness of these thoughts will you be able to take them captive.

Describe your trigger here giving just the facts: who, what, when, where. Do not explain why or give your opinion about the situation. Simply describe it objectively.

In the moment when your trigger occurred, what were your thoughts? Remember, record what you were *thinking,* not what you were feeling. List each thought in the order it occurred, as best you can recall.
Thought 1:

Thought 2:

Thought 3:

Thought 4:

Now, identify your reactions. What did you do or say—or not do and not say—in response to the thoughts that were brought on by your trigger? Or...what did you feel?

Reaction 1 (emotion or action):

Reaction 2 (emotion or action):

Reaction 3 (emotion or action):

Reaction 4 (emotion or action):

Take a look at your thoughts again. Which thought(s) led to each reaction? You should be able to directly trace each of your actions or emotions back to at least one thought.

This exercise is one you can practice over and over again to build awareness of your thoughts and how they influence your reactions. When you find yourself reacting in counterproductive ways, identify the thoughts behind those words or actions.

Ultimately, you want to gain this awareness so you can act immediately to consciously change your thoughts—replacing counterproductive ones—in order to change how you feel and react. When you understand and master your thought life, you'll clear the way to take action and move forward, even in the face of challenges.

It requires self-control and discipline, but changing your thoughts will change your life.

WHAT'S YOUR THINKING STYLE?

In order to effectively replace counterproductive thoughts with those that will propel you forward, you need to be aware of your own thinking style, the filter through which you tend to view yourself, your circumstances, and the world around you. Because the road to your destination will inevitably include at least a few more unexpected turns, it is imperative that you take note of how you interpret the negative events in your life.

Resilient people have learned to explain disappointing, even devastating, events in a way that strengthens their resolve rather than weakening it. By contrast, those who interpret events in a way that leaves them feeling defeated, hopeless, or helpless compromise their ability to recover from setbacks and move forward.

Resilient People Know. . .

Looking at the bright side makes a difference. Optimists live longer, have stronger immune systems, and choose to persevere. Research shows pessimists fail more frequently, are less likely to take action in the face of setbacks, and are more likely to become depressed.[2]

Let's consider a basic disappointment that could happen to just about anyone: failing your first college exam. What would you tell yourself if this happened to you?

A student with a pessimistic thinking style would tend to interpret the event as a personal failure, seeing permanent implications that pervade every area of her life. Her thoughts might include, *I'm obviously not as smart as I thought I was* (personal), followed by, *Maybe I'm just not cut out for college* (permanent), followed by, *I can't get anything right. I'm always failing. I bet I'm going to fail in my other classes too* (general catastrophizing). Concluding she's not smart and not cut out for college gives her an excuse for future failure. She's already determined that she doesn't have what it takes to succeed, so where is her motivation to study harder next time?

Another student who approaches the same disappointment—failing the first test of the semester—with an optimistic thinking style will look for evidence to help him make sense of the situation. If he studied and prepared well, he will likely conclude there was a grading error or that he did not grasp the material as well as he thought he had. He will be honest with himself about other contributing factors. His thoughts will lead him to take positive action: *This is frustrating because the test covered a lot of reading material that was not emphasized in class* (external), followed by, *This is just one test—I have five more opportunities to get my grade back up* (temporary), followed by, *Next time, I will focus my studies more on the reading assignments and instead of just one night of study, I think I'd better prepare to study two or three nights before a test* (specific). A person with this thinking style explains negative events by looking at the external causes, not just the personal ones. He sees negative events as a phase rather than a permanent state. And he interprets the events in a way that pinpoints specific reasons for the problem, refusing to allow one failure or mistake to spill into other, unrelated areas. This frees him to pursue practical solutions rather than getting stuck in regret and failure.

How Will You Think About Your Life?

We all have tests in life. You're going through one right now—and the results carry much more weight than any test you took in school. Nonetheless, the principles are the same. Using an optimistic thinking style to interpret your situation will yield strikingly different results from those reached using a pessimistic thinking style.

Dr. Martin Seligman is a renowned psychologist and researcher at the University of Pennsylvania who identified these different styles of explaining our circumstances to ourselves. He calls them "explanatory styles." In the 1960s and '70s, he also pioneered the research on a phenomenon known as *learned helplessness*. According to him, those who give up do so because they don't think they can do anything to improve the outcome of a situation. He wrote in his book *Learned Optimism:*

> Your habitual way of explaining bad events, your explanatory
> [thinking] style, is more than just the words you mouth when

you fail. It is a habit of thought, learned in childhood and adolescence. Your explanatory style stems directly from your view of your place in the world—whether you think you are valuable and deserving, or worthless and hopeless. It is the hallmark of whether you are an optimist or a pessimist.[3]

The Bible confirms the power our thinking styles hold over the rest of our lives. Proverbs 23:7 says, "As he thinks in his heart, so *is* he" (NKJV).

Your thinking style can be a powerful tool for bouncing back, or it can be a trap that keeps you stuck—not just for days or weeks but for years. So let's take a look at your thinking style. How do you explain your most recent setback—from an optimistic vantage point or an entrenched pessimistic perspective?

As you think about what you've lost—money, job, marriage, home, health, whatever it is—do you see this event in your life as a personal failure? In other words, do you hold yourself fully responsible for what has happened in your life, or were factors beyond your control involved?

_____ Yes, I am entirely at fault.

_____ No, external factors also contributed to my disappointment or loss.

If you answered yes, take a moment to identify specifically what you did to cause this negative event to occur. Write a complete list of your actions here. If you need more room, write about it in your journal. When you are done, ask yourself, *What have I learned and how will I use these lessons in the future?*

If you believe that external factors were at play in your loss, identify what those external factors were. Take this opportunity to reflect on the circumstances beyond your control.

Do you see this loss as permanent or temporary? In other words, at some point in the future, do you believe you will be able to satisfactorily recover what you have lost or regain a similar level of success? Remember, you define success for you. Setbacks can cause us to reevaluate what matters most, so our values and goals may change. You may decide that your life in the future doesn't have to look exactly as it did in the past in order for you to achieve a full comeback. So again, the question is, Do you see your loss as permanent or temporary?

_____ Permanent
_____ Temporary

Is your setback an isolated problem, or does it carry over to numerous other areas of your life? In other words, do you believe this event is merely one manifestation of a flaw or weakness that permeates your efforts in every area of your life?

_____ Yes, this negative event is just one example of a bigger flaw.
_____ No, this event is specific and isolated.

Moving from Helpless to Hopeful

Take another look at your answers in the previous section. While they are not conclusive, your answers can reveal important truths about how you tend to think about your situation. If you believe that the challenge you face right now is entirely your fault, it will last forever, and it will undermine every area of your life, then there is really no point in trying to bounce back, is there? After all, if your challenge is permanent and you have no way to positively affect your future, why bother trying?

This is an example of learned helplessness, and it's a dangerous place to linger. It leads to giving up, accepting life in the ditch as your new home, and not even bothering to improve your circumstances by making the choices that are within your control. Certainly, no matter your personal thinking style, you will have moments when negative thoughts flood your mind. You may sometimes feel hopeless and helpless. But that doesn't mean you *are* helpless, nor is your situation without hope.

I completely understand that your particular circumstance may mean your life truly has changed forever. If someone you love has died, the painful truth is that you can do nothing to bring that person back. But it doesn't mean the pain will always be this intense. It doesn't mean your life no longer has purpose. Surely, your loved one would want to see you living fully rather than remaining stuck for years without joy or emotional healing.

As you look at the turn your life has taken, remember that, while some aspects may be permanent, other aspects of your circumstances are changeable. This is where your hope must lie. Your helplessness can become hopefulness as you listen for clues about how to move purposefully along your new path. Remember that resilient people reach out. They epitomize the Serenity Prayer we talked about in chapter 5:

> *God, grant me the serenity*
> *To accept the things I cannot change,*

Courage to change the things I can,
And wisdom to know the difference.

Hopefulness comes, in part, by mustering the courage to change what you can.

In Natalie's case, that means changing her approach to relationships. It means being honest about her fears so she can address them. It means learning some of the relationship skills she was never exposed to growing up. It means choosing not to repeat her mother's mistakes—or her father's. Natalie would do well to reach out to others who can help her learn these skills, confront her fears, and welcome and keep love in her life. She might coach herself with questions such as: Who do I know in a solid, healthy marriage? Could they mentor me and help me better identify what I need to do differently? Where could I go for individual counseling or coaching? What fears is it time for me to conquer?

If you lean toward an optimistic thinking style, bouncing back will be easier. But don't be discouraged if your thinking style tends to be more pessimistic. Optimism can be learned. Through the power of God working in you and your willingness to change, you can begin thinking in ways that are more productive and positive. You can develop and own the mind-set that "with God all things are possible" (Matthew 19:26). It's true. No matter what lies ahead, you will move through life with more peace, meaning, and effectiveness if your thoughts are filled with faith and hope than if you feed your mind a steady diet of negativity and despair.

Romans 12:2 urges us, "Do not conform to the pattern of this world, but be transformed by the renewing of your mind." Renewing your mind is a continual process of nurturing a thinking style that affirms your belief in a future of purpose and hope.

You Have Everything You Need

Use the Power of Your *Thoughts*

Practice the Trigger ➔ Thoughts ➔ Reactions exercise to build awareness about your thoughts. Specifically focus on identifying triggers that cause you to lose your motivation and prevent you from moving forward.

Use the Power of Your *Words*

You may have counterproductive thoughts, but you do not have to verbalize them. Do your best not to use your words against you. Remember, "The tongue has the power of life and death" (Proverbs 18:21).

Use the Power of Your *Actions*

Remember, by changing your thoughts, you can change your actions. If you're feeling unmotivated or frustrated, notice what you are thinking. Then choose to replace that thinking with thoughts that strengthen and inspire you to action.

Use the Power of *Relationships*

Try the Trigger ➔ Thoughts ➔ Reactions exercise with a friend or loved one. Having someone else ask questions to help you clarify your thoughts can be an effective way to build awareness.

Use the Power of *Prayer*

Lord, I want my thoughts to be Your thoughts. Help me think productive thoughts. Help me think clearly so I can address the issues that are within my control while rejecting lies and discouragement that are not from You. Give me the wisdom and self-awareness to take every thought captive so I am strong for the battle ahead. Amen.

Triumph Over Trials: Ronetta's Story

In 2010 I had the privilege of hearing Ronetta Slaughter at a Resilient Women's Conference. As she shared her story of a faith that endured through monumental pain and loss, there wasn't a dry eye in the sanctuary.

A few months later I enjoyed the opportunity to speak with Ronetta one on one. "When did life stop going the way you planned it?" I asked. She laughed, then answered, "When I was four. Do you have awhile?"

That's when I learned that the resilient attitude she'd demonstrated as an adult, and which she'd shared with us at the conference, had its roots in a difficult childhood. Ronetta was four years old when her mother died suddenly of an asthma attack, an event that changed her life forever. Just two months later, Ronetta's father married a woman with whom he'd been having an affair prior to his wife's death and who was carrying his child.

"My siblings and I had to deal with the wicked stepmother syndrome," Ronetta recalls of the mistreatment she endured. Between their tough Brooklyn neighborhood, alcoholic father, and unkind stepmother, Ronetta and her siblings had a lot to overcome. But her maternal grandmother, who lived in the same building, nurtured her grandchildren with love and positivity. "My grandmother never said a harsh word about my father and stepmother," she remembers. "I think that really helped us persevere through some of the difficulties we had growing up."

Ronetta seems to be a walking, breathing confirmation of the research that suggests some people build up a sort of mental toughness through childhood challenges, a strength that enables them to withstand adversity in adulthood. She was a wife and mother of two in June 1997 when her six-year-old son, Anthony, was diagnosed with a brain tumor. The following June, her husband, Wayne, was killed by a drunk driver on I-85 in Atlanta. Wayne had pulled onto the shoulder to check a suspicious noise his truck was making. The collision knocked his body into an onslaught of moving vehicles traveling the interstate.

"When they told me Wayne had been killed, I was standing near a wall at work," she says. "I remember screaming and just sliding down the wall. I was in shock."

Wayne and Ronetta had been active at Victory World Church in Atlanta, and their church family was extremely supportive. Wayne had led Ronetta to the Lord years earlier, and now she relied on that faith day by day. Anthony was constantly in and out of the hospital for brain surgeries, radiation, and other treatments. On several occasions, they thought he wouldn't make it, but he was a fighter and kept bouncing back.

Four men, fellow church members and friends of Wayne, provided constant support. Ronetta says, "The doctors would ask, 'Which of you is Anthony's father?' And they said, 'We all are.' After Wayne died, they just picked up the mantle covering our family."

But Anthony's problems didn't get better. He was diagnosed with diabetes. He lost his sight in one eye and had limited sight in the other. "He fought for a long time," Ronetta says. But in January 2006, her son died.

How does a wife and mother recover from such devastating losses?

"No matter what things look like in the natural, that was not where I was to keep my eyes," she explains. "If I kept my eyes focused on the things I was seeing, I would not be functioning right now." In other words, Ronetta Slaughter had hope and faith. Hebrews 11:1 says, "Faith is the substance of things hoped for, the evidence of things not seen" (NKJV).

So how did Ronetta maintain her faith through her darkest times?

She decided to focus on gratitude and look back over her life to take note of the hand of God guiding and protecting her from childhood on. "With all the things that have happened, I could have been in a much worse place," she acknowledges. "I could see that God has been in my life."

One of the biggest hurdles she had to overcome was constantly asking, "'Why? Why can't I have my son? Everyone else's son is graduating. Why did this happen to me?' God spoke to me and said, 'Why Mary? Why Jesus? Why Moses?' and I decided to stop asking.

"I came to the conclusion," she continued, "that if I stayed in the whys and why nots, those questions would lead me to thoughts that would keep me in bondage. The truth is, no one can ever answer those questions, so why would I stay there?" Ronetta understood that by spending too much time trying to explain our disappointments, we can get stuck in a cycle of bitterness—and possibly miss out on the blessings yet to come.

In late 2006, a blessing walked into Ronetta's life. She began dating a friend she'd known for five years. A year later, they were engaged. She invited her stepmother, the woman who had mistreated her and her siblings when they were growing up, to light the candle as the mother of the bride at the wedding ceremony. Not long after, they had an opportunity to talk on the phone, and Ronetta says it was the first time in the thirty-nine years her stepmother had been married to her father that she ever remembers their having a heart-to-heart conversation. Her stepmother apologized "the best she knew how," Ronetta says, and said, "*I love you*" that night. "The Lord wiped away my unforgiveness. I forgave her." Her stepmother died in her sleep that same night—and Ronetta had the blessing of knowing all was right between the two of them.

Ronetta and her new love, Andre, married two weeks later. "I *love* where I am today," she says with a smile. "It is a place of peace and joy and unexplainable love. I absolutely love my life right now." It might sound odd, she says. "I miss my son, but I don't miss having to take care of an ill son. He is healed and excited, running around in heaven. Peace is where I am right now, for the first time in my life." Ronetta says if she could change one thing, she would go back and go to college. So after all these years, she is doing just that.[4]

Ronetta's Lessons from the Ditch

- If I can get through losing my husband and son, I know you can get through your setback too. You really can if you just make the choice in your heart and your head. The mind will take you all sorts of places, and you must learn to take your negative thoughts captive.

- Everybody goes through stuff. The question is, How are you going to deal with it? Are you going to crack or bounce back?

- If you have lost something—whether a loved one, a job, your savings, whatever—be grateful that you had it. Be grateful for the experience. Then be thankful for the opportunity that lies before you today.

- The only thing we can control is our emotions and how much faith and trust we have in the Lord. Decide to stand and press through it. If you keep standing, the

Lord is faithful to redeem everything that the enemy has taken. I am living proof. I have an awesome husband, a beautiful daughter, and my son is with the Lord. I have lost nothing.

ELEVEN

Why Don't You Feel Happier by Now?

*Reclaiming Your Joy
Even Before Your Comeback Is Complete*

- *Find daily reasons to rejoice.*

- *Build a bank account of positive emotions.*

- *Be intentional in your pursuit of joy.*

Stacy has always had a passion for real estate. Not only is she a licensed real estate agent, but during the real estate boom, she made a killing buying and flipping properties. She acquired three rental properties that she intended to sell—just around the time the real estate market took a dive. Instead of making a profit, she found herself upside down on every single property she owned while her income from real estate clients dwindled by about 80 percent. Tenants on two of the rental properties had to be evicted for nonpayment, which meant she was stuck with the full cost of her mortgage payments while the disputes were tied up in the small-claims court system.

Although Stacy has been good at making money, she admittedly has a poor track record of keeping it. So when her income dried up, she didn't have resources to fall back on. To make things worse, she initially dealt with her frustration with retail therapy.

Now, almost three years after she took action to get herself out of the ditch, Stacy is close to meeting her financial and personal goals. In the process of reining in her emotional spending, paying down debt, and starting to save, she has transformed her mental attitude about money. If she had not come so close to losing everything, she doesn't believe she would have ever changed her attitude.

However, Stacy is now dealing with a new problem. Although she's making great progress, she isn't feeling as happy as she thought she would. "I feel more confident about my ability to handle money," she says. "And I also realize I don't need nearly as much 'stuff' as I thought I did—and that has been liberating. But now I feel much more aware of other changes I'd like to make in my life. So much of my energy the last couple of years has been consumed with getting back on track financially. I think I assumed that once I solved that issue all would be well. Instead, now that I'm out of that ditch, I see more issues I need to address."

Stacy's predicament isn't unusual. It takes a great deal of courage and energy to bounce back from a setback. After navigating your way back to an old path or onto a new one, the happiness you anticipated may still be elusive. We tend to expect that once we get back to where we were—or at least get out of the ditch and onto a purposeful path—the pain, frustration, or disappointment should be nothing more than a memory.

While things may have improved significantly since that moment you found yourself in the ditch, the fact remains that your life will never be exactly the same as before your setback and you cannot regain the time lost. You may encounter frequent reminders of former relationships, of opportunities you can't reclaim, of how different things might have been—and those reminders can tempt you to feel sorry for yourself. Comparing your milestones on this new journey with the accomplishments prior to your setback is counterproductive. If you insist on using your former life as a point of reference for measuring your progress, you set yourself up to be discouraged. But if, instead, your point of reference is the ditch, each small step forward from that starting place is a blessing to celebrate, a reason to rejoice.

The elusiveness of joy might also result from realizing that your old life wasn't as satisfying as you had expected. Even though you may now be intentionally living in ways that are more closely aligned with your true priorities, you may feel a sadness about having spent more years than you'd like to admit pursuing a life that didn't bring joy and fulfillment. But in ruminating on time wasted, you'll only lose more time. So instead of beating yourself up, be thankful that getting thrown off course gave you the opportunity to choose a new path before any more time was lost.

Expectations that are not aligned with reality can be another source of disappointment. Disappointment can always be traced to unmet expectations. I am not suggesting you lower your expectations, but rather that you make adjustments. Instead of being continually disappointed and frustrated that your recovery isn't happening as quickly as you'd like, adjust your expectations to a more realistic time line, even giving yourself some margin for error. Remember that recovery is a process, and it usually takes more time than we expect or want. But in the end, it is the result of the process that matters, not how long it has taken.

Think of it like this: Some babies learn to walk at ten months old, while others take much longer to achieve that milestone. But can you imagine a mother giving up on her child because, in her judgment, the learning process was taking too long? Of course not! We would find it odd and appalling for a parent to get angry at a child and declare, "Quit trying. Obviously, you're not going to get this. Just keep crawling." Parents thoroughly enjoy watching little Johnny figure out how to take one step after the other until finally he figures out how to walk without stumbling or falling. Although the end result is what matters, the parents and child find joy in the process as well.

You too can find joy in the process of making your comeback. You may never be happy about the difficulty or disappointment you've endured, but you can take joy in how God is using it to shape you and to lead you toward something better.

The fact that you are here—that you've made it to this point at all—is an excellent reason to rejoice. Psalm 118:24 says, "This is the day the LORD has made; we will rejoice and be glad in it" (NKJV). What can you rejoice about? No matter how bad your situation, you surely have something for which to be grateful, something to rejoice about. Coach yourself toward gratitude with a few questions:

What is the best thing that happened today?

What can I look forward to today?

What beautiful or interesting thing can I marvel at today?

Who am I most grateful for in this moment and why?

In what way do I see God's presence in my life today?

What material possession (a bed, car, and so on) makes my life a little more comfortable today?

THE POWER OF A POSITIVE PERSPECTIVE

Our culture places a high value on happiness—often using it as the ultimate measure of whether or not we've arrived at a place of true success. Most of the goals we pursue—better relationships, career growth, money, weight loss, or even a recovery from a setback—we pursue because we believe they will bring us greater happiness. But in general the kind of happiness our culture seeks tends to be extremely shallow, based on outward accomplishments, material acquisitions, titles, and status. And as we've learned from the painful experience of our setbacks, such external things can quickly disappear.

I firmly believe God wants us to be happy, but the happiness He offers is a more meaningful, deeper experience of joy that does not depend on circumstances. Ecclesiastes 3:12–13 says, "There is nothing better for people than to be happy and to do good while they live. That each of them may eat and drink, and find satisfaction in all their toil—this is the gift of God."

Indeed, it is a beautiful gift to feel joy. It may seem irrelevant or even insensitive for me to suggest that you can experience joy while you're still in the midst of recovery. Actually, I'm convinced that, right now, it's more important than ever for you to have joy on a daily basis. Of course, it would be inauthentic for you to pretend to be ecstatic and having fun while pressing through one of the most difficult times of your life. That's not what I'm talking about. I'm talking about finding joy in the little things— those seemingly insignificant things that, in the grand scheme of life, add up to quite a lot. It's the melodic sound of birds chirping in the morning, the burst of flavor when you bite into your next meal, the comforting touch of someone who cares about you, the chance to help someone else, or the e-mail that just came through encouraging you to persevere. I'm also talking about finding joy in each small step of progress toward your recovery, such as getting a lead on a job opening or paying off a debt or sticking with your diet for a full week.

Each time you find a reason to rejoice, no matter how small, you increase your inner strength for the next stage of your comeback.

The Bible repeatedly affirms this connection between joy and strength for daily living. The prophet Nehemiah wrote in the Old Testament, "The joy of the LORD is your strength" (Nehemiah 8:10). King

Solomon alluded to it when he said, "A cheerful heart is good medicine, but a crushed spirit dries up the bones" (Proverbs 17:22).

The connection between a joyful perspective and resilience in adversity also is a foundational finding in a number of psychological studies. Research spearheaded by Dr. Barbara Fredrickson at the University of North Carolina has confirmed all sorts of physical and mental benefits that are derived from positive emotion.[1] Let's look at just a few.

Positive Emotion Expands Your Ability to Deal with Adversity and Stress

Positive emotion creates chemical changes in the brain and body that enable you to better cope with stress.[2]

Ever had a bad day and then overreacted to a small incident—say, someone cut you off in traffic or a loved one said something you didn't like? Later, you looked back and realized you could have handled it better, but it felt as if someone had tweaked your last nerve. Now, imagine that same adversity taking place on a joyful day. You just had a good laugh with a friend, your boss congratulated you for your great work on a project, and you worked out this morning just like you said you would. Soon after you arrived home at the end of the day, a loved one made an insensitive or harsh comment. How do you respond? You may be annoyed, but you probably won't lose your temper. Because all those positive experiences have expanded your emotional resources, small adversities aren't likely to prompt a strong reaction.

The same holds true when you face big adversities. The more positive emotion you have—in the form of laughter, good conversation, fun and playtime (yes, adults need playtime!), gratitude, prayer, and savoring the simple pleasures of life—the better and faster you'll be able to bounce back.

Positive Emotion Enhances Your Ability to Think Effectively

Research shows that experiencing a positive emotion—for example, laughing at a funny television show—increases a person's effectiveness in completing tasks, such as recalling information, remembering faces, or rationalizing decisions. Likewise, negative experiences cause us to focus more on negative events or feelings and make us more likely to ignore the positive. Negative emotion actually narrows your thinking so you begin to only see other negatives.

Ever gotten into a disagreement with someone, and suddenly you recall everything that person has done wrong for the last five years? The little habits or comments that didn't bother you before suddenly seem unbearable. The person still has many positive qualities, but the negative emotion makes it more difficult for you to see the positive. If you were making a decision about how to handle the disagreement, doing so immediately following the disagreement could be a mistake. The negative emotion impairs your judgment. Wait a little while and then address it. Your decisions will be more thoughtful and rational. This is really important to remember at this time in your life. You have crucial decisions to make. Responding from a negative frame of mind could be detrimental to your long-term future. Especially avoid making significant decisions after a particularly frustrating encounter; you are likely to regret your choice later. Intentionally putting yourself in a positive frame of mind helps ensure you make solid decisions.

Positive Emotions Build over Time—Like a Bank Account

I know the idea that you can actually store up positive emotions sounds a little far-fetched, but research shows it is absolutely true. When you build up positive emotional experiences over time, it becomes a resource you can draw on in times of trouble.

Think about two people in your life. Friend A is the person you most enjoy being around. He or she is positive and encouraging, funny and easygoing. You love being around Friend A. You've built trust and a positive communication with each other. Now think of Friend B, someone you do not enjoy being around. This person is negative and pessimistic. Communication with him or her is often strained. Spending time with Friend B leaves you exhausted.

Over time, your relationship with Friend A has built up a lot of positive emotion. If and when you hit a rough patch with that friend, the trust and goodwill built over time will likely help you recover. In fact, the bonds of a good relationship tend to grow stronger after you work through adversity. But the same is likely not true of Friend B. The negative aspects of your relationship have drained it of the resources needed to cope with a misunderstanding or serious disagreement. In fact, your connection is so vulnerable that a single rough patch could destroy the relationship altogether.

A similar pattern occurs when it comes to inner resilience. Those who have experienced minimal positive emotion in their lives often take longer to recover from their setbacks. By contrast, positive emotion experienced over time builds a cushion to protect you from the impact of a fall. When life takes an unexpected turn, you may get knocked off your path and into a ditch, but rather than landing on concrete, you will land on a soft, grassy patch. You may still be hurt and disoriented, but you will recover with fewer injuries.

If you have children, you may want to keep in mind that creating a loving, supportive environment for them now is a way to build their long-term emotional bank account. Like the rest of humanity, they will inevitably face adversities of their own. Give them the gift of a soft, cushiony patch to land on.

Resilient People Know . . .

Positive emotions broaden and build, meaning they expand your capacity to handle adversity, decisions, and stress — and they build up over time. The more positive emotion you experience in the long term (good relationships, joy, humor, gratitude), the thicker the cushion that protects you when you fall.[3]

YOUR RECIPE FOR JOY

One other key finding of Dr. Fredrickson's research is that negative emotions are more powerful than positive, by a ratio of 3:1.[4] In other words, it takes at least three positive experiences to counteract the effects of one negative interaction or emotion.

While we can deliberately choose to seek reasons to rejoice, it's impossible to entirely avoid negativity—particularly when you're still recovering from a setback. At times, you might feel bombarded with negative thoughts and emotions. And, of course, any given day may include encounters with difficult, negative people and/or the navigation of extremely challenging conversations and situations. To counter the impact of negative interactions and thoughts, it's important to intentionally seek out relief through the positive.

So let's look at the key ingredients you can use to create a nourishing recipe to daily feed more joy into your life and strengthen you for this journey. Researcher Dr. Sonja Lyubomirsky posits that while about 50 percent of our happiness levels are set, based on temperament and personality, the other 50 percent is changeable. Just 10 percent of happiness is attributable to your circumstances, according to Lyubomirsky, while a full 40 percent is attributable to the intentional activities you choose.[5] You can't change the genes you were born with, and you can't always control your circumstances. However, you can control your choices and actions day to day.

Let's consider a few of the choices and actions you can take to build more positive emotion into your life:

1. Keep a Gratitude Journal

Gratitude is one of the characteristics most closely associated with happiness. So count your blessings before bed and when you wake up. At the beginning of the day ask, What do I choose to look forward to? Followed by, Why am I looking forward to it? At the end of the day, ask, What was the best thing about today? Or, What am I most grateful for and why? To get the most benefit out of your gratitude journal, identify the blessing *and* reflect for a moment on what the blessing means to you and why it is important. Gratitude helps you focus on the good that is present in your life rather than being preoccupied with what's missing. And research shows that counting your blessings regularly for just three weeks can have measurable health effects, such as a stronger immune system.[6]

When you have particularly bad days, that's when it's most helpful to count your blessings. Or boost your spirits by pulling out your journal to read what you've written on better days.

2. Seek the Meaning

God is a God of purpose. Every experience offers lessons and opportunities for growth. In the next chapter we'll look more closely at what it means to grow through adversity. In the meantime, please believe that, however unpleasant the process, this turning point in your life can hold meaning that shapes you for the better. This can be particularly difficult when circumstances seem utterly unfair, when the pain results from the choices of others or from some seemingly random twist of fate. But even in such instances, God can grow you and teach you. He can work all things together for your ultimate good.

God is speaking to you, even in the midst of your frustration and fear. Listen for the message, and watch for the purpose in your pain.

3. Choose Hope

Hope is a prerequisite for faith. "Faith is the substance of things hoped for, the evidence of things not seen" (Hebrews 11:1, NKJV). Hope is what pulls you forward in the face of difficult odds. When you stop hoping, you start settling—settling for less than God promised you and accepting disappointment as your destiny. *It is not.*

What are you hoping for? Write it down. Keep it in front of you and cling to it. If you hope, then it means you believe it is possible. And "everything is possible for one who believes" (Mark 9:23).

4. Move Your Body

Did you know that, for many people, exercise can be as effective as antidepressants? I can hear you through these pages saying to me, "Valorie, I don't get positive emotion from exercising. I get no joy there!" Actually, you do.

When you exercise, your body releases mood-enhancing endorphins that create positive feelings in the body. These endorphins diminish the perception of pain, improve sleep, release your muscle tension, and reduce cortisol, the hormone produced when you are under stress. Some studies, such as one conducted by Duke University researchers, show that aerobic exercise can be equally as effective as antidepressants in fighting depression, particularly as a long-term solution to symptoms of a major depressive episode.[7]

Depression is a common experience for those going through a setback, but it isn't inevitable. If your health permits, get some type of exercise daily. Medical experts say thirty minutes of exercise three to five times a week is the minimum necessary to see long-term effects in combating depression and other illnesses. But even small amounts of exercise, such as a brisk fifteen-minute walk, can boost your mood in the short-term. (Please note: By no means am I suggesting you ignore symptoms of depression. If you find yourself unable to shake feelings of sadness or have difficulty sleeping for more than two weeks, please see your doctor right away and consider talking to a trained therapist.)

5. Connect

Throughout life, not just in crisis, strong relationships empower you to thrive. In my interviews with those who've come back strong after major setbacks, many cited a child or other loved one as the source of their inspiration and tenacity. "I had to make it. They needed me," was a repeated comment. But strong connections to others and support from them also play a major role in making a comeback. "I had never needed help from anyone," one man noted after losing his life savings through divorce and a business failure. "I was always the one giving the help. But now, with limited income, I could not turn down the generosity of others."

The power of relationships isn't just about needing others for motivation or material help, however. Relationships provide connection, a source of positive emotion, and keep you from being isolated and overwhelmed by the sheer work of making a comeback on your own. Consider Solomon's words in Ecclesiastes 4:9–12:

> *Two are better than one,*
> > *because they have a good return for their labor:*

If either of them falls down,
      one can help the other up.
But pity anyone who falls
      and has no one to help them up!
Also, if two lie down together, they will keep warm.
      But how can one keep warm alone?
Though one may be overpowered,
      two can defend themselves.
A cord of three strands is not quickly broken.

Although you may feel an impulse to withdraw socially, resist the temptation. Now more than ever, you need to connect with positive, encouraging people.

As you deliberately choose to tap into healthy relationships, it's wise to also limit your exposure to relationships that stir up negativity or leave you feeling discouraged. You may not be able to eliminate every challenging relationship (after all, your sister isn't going to stop being your sister even if she drains your energy), but you can be intentional about limiting your time with people who will make it harder for you to bounce back. Most important, you can be intentional about strengthening bonds with positive, optimistic people in your life, who will help offset the effects of negative interactions.

6. Give
This may seem counterintuitive, but finding a way to share your resources with someone else is a significant source of positive emotion. Doing something for others helps us see the power we have to effect change. It can help put life into perspective. As dark as your situation may seem, there are other people struggling who have even fewer resources, less hope, or problems you can be grateful are not yours to bear. Look for

opportunities to help them—or to at least help somebody. Use what you have to bless others, whether with an encouraging word, a smile, a donation, or whatever meaningful gift God prompts you to offer. Being a blessing blesses you too. *Well-doing* increases your *well-being*.[8]

7. Make Time for Prayer and Meditation

This seventh ingredient is tremendously powerful. God wants to hear from you (prayer) and He also wants to speak to you (meditation). Amazingly, more than one thousand scientific studies on meditation show that it yields numerous health benefits, including:

- Reducing negative emotions
- Creating a sense of calm in the midst of stress
- Increasing self-awareness
- Improving brain function

When you take time to wait "in silence for God" (Psalm 62:1, NASB), you will hear Him speaking in ways that remind you that He is your rock, your refuge—and that you don't need to be shaken by the storms of life.

Take time daily to pray and meditate. Pray not only for your own situation, but also be sure to broaden your prayers to include the needs of others, thereby putting your own circumstances into perspective.

INVITE JOY INTO YOUR LIFE

Soon after my marriage ended, I found myself doing something I hadn't done in more than fifteen years: running. I had always been a walker, but now running became my solace—a timely metaphor for stretching beyond my comfort zone.

Before that summer, I'd been quick to say I hated running. But here I was doing it—and actually enjoying it. I began to notice that on days when I didn't go to the track I felt a bit off kilter, and my thoughts drifted more toward fear of the future rather than faith. I began ruminating on things that had happened and found myself becoming angry more easily. But a three-mile run renewed my energy and gave me a chance to pray and meditate on my belief that my future would be better, not worse.

I also kept a gratitude journal and purposely pondered all the things for which I was grateful, despite the fact that my life wasn't going the way I planned it. And I began asking God to show me the message in my circumstances. What lesson was He offering me? What message was He trying to get through?

As I took a few tentative steps along my new path, I gained immense joy from being around family. Joy came from long walks and talks—sometimes with God, sometimes with family. Joy came in knowing that God was with me. Joy came in meditating on His Word. Joy came in giving myself permission to not have all the answers. By being in a supportive environment, I had the chance to talk about what I was going through and to process it. It was a healthy step that fortified me for the road ahead.

Now this doesn't mean that I didn't have any sad days. In fact, I gave myself permission to cry when the emotion hit me. But I didn't wallow in it. Would I have cried more if I had tried to get through that period of my life alone? If I had chosen not to be around people who love me and whom I love? If I had stayed cooped up in my house refusing to go outside or exercise or do anything fun? Absolutely. I believe it would have prolonged my recovery and left me feeling isolated and depressed. My three-month transition strengthened me for the bigger steps that lay ahead as I figured out what my new life would look like and began to embrace it with hope and joy.

What about you? The joy of the Lord is your strength too. As you continue to forge ahead, I encourage you to be intentional about inviting joy into your life, in whatever form the Lord delivers it.

You Have Everything You Need

Use the Power of Your *Thoughts*

Think for a moment about what causes you to feel disappointment or a lack of joy in this stage of your comeback. What specifically do you think about that brings on these feelings? How could you change your expectations or thoughts in order to create a greater sense of contentment and peace with where you are?

Use the Power of Your *Words*

Identify someone to whom you are grateful. Write that person a "gratitude letter," detailing the specific act(s) for which you are grateful, what it meant to you, and why you feel compelled to say thank-you now.

Use the Power of Your *Actions*

Look at the seven ingredients for joy in this chapter. Choose one that you are not currently doing and begin implementing it in the next twenty-four hours.

Use the Power of *Relationships*

Rather than mailing or e-mailing your gratitude letter, choose a time and place to read the letter aloud to the recipient. Whether over dinner or during a long-distance phone call, give that individual the pleasure of hearing the words directly from you.

Use the Power of *Prayer*

Lord, I pray that out of Your glorious riches You will strengthen me with power through Your Spirit in my inner being (Ephesians 3:16). Help me find joy in the little things. Grant me the discipline to accomplish what I need to

*do and the attitude to persevere. Your Word says to consider it pure joy when-
ever I face trials of many kinds, because the testing of my faith produces perseverance. Help me to endure, knowing that perseverance must finish its work
so that I may be mature and complete, not lacking anything (James 1:2–4).
Lord, I don't want to lack anything. I don't like what I am going through, but
I will choose joy in the midst of it because I believe You have a plan for me. I
am choosing to trust You, Lord. Grow me and shape me into the person
You've always meant for me to be. Amen.*

Triumph Over Trials: Ruth's Story

Ruth Puleo's darkest hour as a parent came when her daughter, Julie, began to suffer intense migraine headaches—so intense Julie had to stop going to school. She missed the rest of her sophomore year of high school and all of her junior and senior years. "Her whole life literally stopped," Ruth says. "I had to try to homeschool her. Fifty percent of the time, she was in bed. Our shades were always pulled down because the light would bother her. We couldn't turn on the TV because the noise was painful."

Ruth grew up as a preacher's kid, and she and her two sisters, Lillian and Faith, all serve in ministry—yet this trial tested her faith. She worked tirelessly to find an answer to her daughter's pain. She took Julie to countless doctors and even tried alternative therapies as well as a faith healer. Nothing seemed to help.

"I was afraid some day I would come home and find her dead. I thought I had failed somehow and that is why Julie wasn't healed." That belief was exacerbated by the comments of people in church who had asked Ruth, "Well, do you think Julie has some sort of secret sin in her life, and this is why she is suffering like this?" Such comments may come out of a sincere concern, Ruth says, but they are misguided. "When people approach you like this, you no longer feel safe."

Ruth says the hardest part about getting knocked into the ditch was that she felt helpless. "I invested so much into my children. I loved them so much. My darkness came from knowing that I could not change this for my daughter. It did not matter what I did." It wasn't the first time Ruth had faced health challenges with one of her children, and it wouldn't be the last. Previously her three-year-old son had nearly died of viral meningitis. When the illness left him paralyzed on the right side and suffering a 106-degree fever, Ruth says she "gave him back to the Lord." He survived without brain damage, and today he is a pastor.

"That trial was a much shorter period of time than Julie's. With Julie, it was a daily thing we faced as a family for over five years. And when you don't have the support of your church family and people think wrongly of your child or your family, where do you go?" Ruth says.

"I got to a point where I sat out on the front porch and couldn't read my Bible. I had loved the Lord all my life—I couldn't remember when I didn't know the Lord. And I asked Him, *'Lord, do You hear me? Will You answer me?'* God said to me, *'Ruth, you do not have to earn my love. I love you unconditionally.'*"

This encounter marked a pivotal moment for Ruth, as she gained a newfound understanding of God's unconditional love. She then took specific faith-filled steps to persevere through this storm.

First, she made the decision to believe God loved her regardless of what trials came her way. Trials were no longer a sign to her that she was doing something wrong. Next, she says she had to accept the story of her life that was being written. She admits it was extremely difficult to watch her daughter's pain and suffering. "It was the first time I felt I knew what depression might be. It was hard to get my feet out of bed in the morning." But believing in God's love and accepting that the story of her life was still unfolding were critical steps that helped her stop trying to control her daughter's fate.

"I cried and I released her. I stopped trying to find answers. I stopped taking her to the doctor. I stopped trying to give her solutions, push her to do things, make her do homework. I let her take responsibility." In retrospect, Ruth admits it was a relief to Julie, who had been stuck with more needles and dragged to more doctors than she cared to remember. Still, letting go was scary for this loving mother.

"Finding an answer had been my pursuit and my focus for so long," Ruth says. "It was like an emptiness to let go of searching for answers. I think when there is a diagnosis that's not going to change, it is a place where you have to die to the dream of their ever being normal." She compares it to the three Hebrew men thrown into the fiery furnace. "They said we know our God *can* deliver us, and we also know He can take us *through* it; but if not, if we die in this furnace, we will serve Him anyway." Ruth asked herself, *If God never heals her, will I still serve the Lord?* Her answer was yes.

Julie did eventually find some relief. Ruth's oldest daughter, Jenny, who was going through medical school and working for a neurologist, suggested a different medication that eased the pain, which in turn gave Julie some emotional relief.

Jenny also suggested Julie leave home for a month to get out of the house. She went to stay with an aunt, who had helped Ruth through a challenging time during her own teen years. Just as she had ministered to Ruth years earlier, this woman ministered to Julie. When Julie returned home, she had the strength and drive to finish her homeschooling. Although her friends had graduated from high school that spring, Julie wasn't done yet. She graduated high school in December of that year and was accepted to North Central College in Minneapolis. There she continued to suffer migraines, though not as intense due to her new medication. And she met her college sweetheart. They married, and when she became pregnant, the miracle came: a hormone shift during pregnancy eliminated her migraines!

Ruth says her ministry changed as a result of her five-year experience supporting Julie's battle with migraines. She always loved people, but before then, when ministering in church, she admits she loved at a distance. "It wasn't until I was willing to tell on myself and be honest and open about my discouragements and hurts that my ministry was transformed." She says when you share transparently, people realize you are human. "It gives them hope," she explains. "They say, 'If my pastor has been through that, then I can get through it. I'm not a bad person because bad things have happened to me. This is life. I can make it.'"[9]

Ruth's Lessons from the Ditch

- *You can choose how to respond.* It is a choice to be resilient. Forgiveness is a choice. Victory is a choice.
- *Your view of God makes all the difference.* Ask yourself, Will you still serve God if you don't get the answer you want? Will you be mad at God? Will you believe He loves others more? If you get angry at God, you shut yourself off from your greatest resource. Just know that He has a different story for each of us. The real question is, Can you accept the story that He is writing for you?
- *Find safe friends.* Connect with people who are godly and spiritual, with whom you can share the depth of your pain and frustration. They won't necessarily have the answers, but they are a safe, comforting place to cry and hurt.
- *Make a decision to give God the glory.*

TWELVE

How Can You Find the Good in All This?

Growing Through Your Trials,
Not Just Going Through Them

I n my favorite movie, *The Color Purple,* there is a scene in which Miss Celie, played by Whoopi Goldberg, finally musters up the courage to leave her abusive husband, Mister, played by Danny Glover. Over a big family dinner, Mister spews verbal insults at Miss Celie, telling her, "You're black, you're poor, you're ugly, you're a woman, you're nothing at all!" Something in Miss Celie finally clicks. She realizes his words are nonsense, and she doesn't have to keep enduring them. She walks out and steps into the back of a yellow convertible driven by a friend.

As the car eases out of the driveway, she snaps back at Mister with a confidence born of persevering through the unfairness

- *Make this a season of growth.*

- *Consider how your story has shaped you for the better.*

- *Use your experience to help others.*

of life: "I'm poor, black. I might even be ugly, but dear God, I'm here! I'm here!"

And so are you. You are here. Though life has dealt you some challenging circumstances, you have not given up or run away. You're here—and I believe there's a reason for that. I'm convinced that, through the adversities of your life, God is developing something valuable in you and through you.

Posttraumatic Growth

For decades, we've known about a phenomenon called posttraumatic stress disorder, or PTSD. This psychological condition is a response to extreme stress. We most often associate it with soldiers who have repeatedly endured intensely traumatic conditions, such as being under attack with their very lives at stake, seeing friends and fellow soldiers killed before their eyes, and dealing with a host of stressors that most of us could never imagine.

But PTSD does not affect only active-duty soldiers. Doctors observe this condition in the aftermath of a variety of traumas, and studies have shown it affects a wide range of individuals from rape victims to children in the inner city who are regularly exposed to crime and drive-by shootings.

In recent years, researchers have begun studying a lesser known effect of trauma—something Dr. Richard Tedeschi and Dr. Lawrence Calhoun termed "posttraumatic growth."[1] In the aftermath of life crisis—some seismic shift in circumstances—some people emerge from the dust stronger than before. According to Tedeschi and Calhoun,

> Posttraumatic growth is reported by persons who have experienced all sorts of difficult, tragic, catastrophic, and horrible

events. At least some persons experiencing widely different traumatic events (e.g., sexual abuse as children, loss of a home in a fire,...the birth of a severely handicapped child, suffering severe injury, sexual assault and rape, being diagnosed with breast cancer, bone marrow transplantation, military combat and captivity, and becoming physically disabled as an adult), report being changed in positive ways by their struggle with trauma.[2]

These survivors say their losses have produced something of value, and studies find that they have an increased sense of their ability to survive and even triumph in the face of adversity.

Without in any way minimizing the pain you have endured, I'm convinced that it is possible, even probable, that, like these survivors, you will be a stronger person with greater depth of character when you emerge on the other side of whatever challenge confronts you right now. In my numerous interviews with those who have faced major setbacks and life challenges, I've found that, in every single instance, the individuals involved stated emphatically that they were better in some way as a result of their experience. This does not mean they would choose to go through it again, but they are able to recognize and acknowledge they gained value from it. They see how they grew as a result, and in many instances, admit that they would not be where they are now if not for the lessons learned and the opportunities that emerged out of less-than-ideal circumstances.

Jacqueline Jakes, speaking of the ten harrowing years following her brain surgery, quoted Shakespeare to me, "Sweet are the uses of adversity."[3] She went on to say, "Out of all that horror came so much good. I became a changed person and a better mother. I became focused and knew what really mattered in life," she said. "I didn't get distracted because I had to work while I could. Satan meant it for evil, but God used it for good."

Reflecting on her experience, she said, "I would never ever want to go through that again, but I wouldn't change it because I wouldn't be here. I don't think I'd be alive. I think it kept me from doing a lot of things I would have done and experimented with."

Those who go through life-changing experiences often develop a greater compassion for other people who are going through challenges. They become less judgmental of others because they realize that life can change in an instant and tough times happen to anyone. You realize the truth of the statement, "There but for the grace of God go I." Through my own setbacks and realizing my need to receive grace from others, I have learned to be more sensitive to opportunities to demonstrate compassion.

Many trauma survivors also find themselves more comfortable with intimacy. Forced to rely on others for help and perhaps even for survival, they no longer live in denial about their need for human connection. Recognizing your dependence on others is scary, but when you accept that truth, your capacity for intimacy is stretched and expanded.

When my mother suffered an aneurysm, she initially endured numerous related physical disabilities, including a bladder that didn't function. The only way she could be relieved was through catheterization. The nurses told me I'd have to learn to do this procedure for her, but I remained in denial for days while she was still in the hospital. Surely, her bladder would begin functioning before she was released. My fear and anxiety were not about the act of learning to catheterize my mother but about the idea that she was in such poor physical condition that she had to rely on me in that way. It made real the significance of her losses, and also highlighted my own loss of having a healthy mom.

Both of us had to learn to live with this new normal. Over time, and with practice, it became a routine part of the recovery. No longer was the catheter a reminder of what was lost. It was simply what we had to do to get her where she needed and wanted to be. After a few months, my mother's bladder began to function again on its own. But now, nearly a decade later, I can see how that one experience expanded my capacity for intimacy.

In what way(s) do you want to be better as a result of the challenges you face? How do you hope to grow?

In what way(s) have you already seen growth? Have others noticed positive shifts and changes? If so, what are they?

EMBRACE YOUR STORY

This process of understanding how you are better as a result of what you've been through helps you see that, while your challenges may be a setback in some ways, they are a push forward in others—especially from a spiritual perspective.

It would not be fair to say that trauma and setbacks are good. They are hard. They are sometimes unfair. They are devastating in many ways. But they may also lead to greater meaning and fulfillment in life. By no means am I suggesting that your life in the aftermath of an earthquake-sized challenge feels happy and carefree. But even so, you can be in a place of peace and faith. Your life can be more authentic and purposeful. And your certainty of who you can count on and what really matters in life will be greatly enhanced.

In her book *Jacqueline's Spiritual Jewels,* Jacqueline Jakes says, "Don't despise your imperfection.... Even in your limp, He is glorified."[4] In other words, behind your limp is a story that sheds light on who you have become as a person, through the power of God working in you. Without that limp, you might not even be here. Your limp can give you credibility. Your limp means you're a survivor. You know what it means to take a hit and keep going.

No Time for Bitterness

In 2008 I finally had the opportunity to travel to Israel for a television show I was co-hosting, *Aspiring Women,* for the Total Living Network. For years, I had wanted to visit the Holy Land and had even prayed for an opportunity to go. I wanted to walk where Jesus walked and see the land that I read about in my Bible. I did that, and it was a transformative experience. But I had an opportunity while I was there for a truly once-in-a-lifetime opportunity: I interviewed a survivor of the Holocaust.

For two hours, I listened as Rena Quint described the horrifying events of her captivity. She was four years old the day the Nazis rounded up all of the neighbors and family in her ghetto in Poland. She clung to her mother's leg, her two brothers walking next to her, as they were herded into a synagogue. Then soldiers began shooting people randomly.

In that moment, something inexplicable occurred.

An uncle quietly opened a nearby door and motioned for Rena to run toward him. She recalls her mother pushing her in his direction, and she imagines that her mother knew it was the only hope for her youngest child's survival. Rena ran toward the door as gunshots flew across the synagogue. Somehow she made it safely to her uncle. She never saw her mother or brothers again.

The uncle whisked her away to her father, who was part of a slave labor camp working in a factory. He hid her for a while, and when she was big enough, he dressed her as a boy so that she would be allowed to work in the factory bringing water to the workers. Eventually, they were rounded up once more; this time they were packed onto boxcars and sent to a concentration camp. When they arrived, the males were separated from the females, so her father asked a woman to please look after Rena. Before they separated, he gave her a few personal items and asked her to hold on to them, promising to find her after the war was over. It was a promise he was never able to fulfill.

The woman in whose care Rena had been left became the first of many mother figures over the next few years. As each disappeared or died, another woman took Rena under her wing. Presumably missing their own children who'd died or been taken from them, women in the concentration camps were quick to care for little ones as their own. Rena described the deplorable conditions—wearing thin pajamas outdoors in freezing cold weather and eating moldy food she initially swore she'd never touch. "There comes a point when you are so hungry, you'll eat anything." The sight of dead, starved bodies became a normal part of her everyday life.

Somehow she survived the concentration camp, and when the Allied forces showed up to free the prisoners at Bergen-Belsen, Rena eventually had the opportunity to come to America with her last "mother." When that woman died, Rena was nine. She recalls being confused as to why so many people showed up for the funeral. *It was just one person,* she thought. *Why are there so many people here and crying?* In her world, she'd seen hundreds dead and buried in mass graves. She'd never even seen a casket.

Listening to how much horror she'd endured, the many reasons she had to be angry and bitter, I asked Rena if she had been able to forgive the Nazis.

She looked at me, perplexed. "I survived," she said with a grateful tone. "The ones they need forgiveness from are the ones who lost their lives." She went on to explain that she didn't have time to be bitter. She was too grateful for the life she had gained. Eventually adopted by a childless couple in New York, Rena went on to marry and have children and, in 1984, moved to Israel.

If Rena Quint can live a fulfilling, prosperous life after having survived six years of the Holocaust, surely you and I can thrive despite the ditches we've been knocked into. It begins with the attitude we choose. Will you be better as a result of your setback—or bitter?

What Does Your Story Reveal?

While your story is surely not as dark and dramatic as Rena's, I hope you'll take time to think back over the events, decisions, and relationships that brought you to where you are today. As you do so, pay special attention to the ways in which you have changed—in your perspective, your capacity for compassion, your priorities, your faith.

You may find it empowering to write your story. Research by Dr. Laura King, professor at the University of Missouri, has shown that writing about both life traumas and life goals can have physical and mental health benefits.[5] Creating your narrative is therapeutic and helps shape how you see your life. Often, the story of your life is divided into "before" and "after"—as defined by the adverse event that threw you off course. You are a different person in the aftermath of this event. Perhaps you are still in the process of transformation, and six months or six years from now, you will be even more different.

While conducting interviews for this book, I noticed ongoing transformation in the perspective of those I spoke with. Most of the interviews were by phone and lasted one to two hours. Although the individuals had taken many of the steps outlined in this book, most had not asked themselves the type of questions I posed. Not only did the conversation affirm the significance of what they'd been through, but it also gave them an opportunity to pause and reflect on key moments, shifts in thinking, and lessons that emerged as they looked back with a bird's-eye view of their circumstances.

As you develop your narrative perspective, my hope is that you will allow your comeback experience to make you better, not bitter. That decision is entirely up to you. Even through the worst of events, you can choose to be better. Eventually, you may share your story, and God can use it to bless and inspire others.

It's Not All About You

A pivotal moment in my own story occurred when it finally dawned on me that my pain and embarrassment, even my growth and recovery, weren't just about me. God would receive glory through my recovery. There's nothing like a comeback to demonstrate the truth of Ephesians 3:20-21:

> Now to him who is able to do immeasurably more than all we ask
> or imagine, according to his power that is at work within us, to
> him be glory…for ever and ever!

But God's power at work within us isn't just about His helping us on our own journeys but about His using us to help others. He wants to use your experience to deepen your ability to love and serve the people He brings into your life.

> ###### *Resilient People Know...*
>
> You can pay it forward by serving and sharing your wisdom. Do something to bless someone else. Well doing promotes well-being.

When you first land in the ditch, the last thing you are thinking about is how your setback will be a blessing to others. Even as you climb out of the ditch and onto your path, the focus is still on you. And when you arrive at the destination you'd dreamed of, the focus is still pretty much entirely about how blessed you are to have made it through. And you are blessed indeed.

But what is the purpose of God's blessing? Is it purely for our enjoyment and gratitude? It can be so much greater than that. We are blessed to be a blessing.

The very purpose of our being is to love—to love God and love others. When one of the Pharisees asked Jesus, "Teacher, which is the greatest commandment in the Law?" Jesus answered him: "'Love the Lord your God with all your heart and with all your soul and with all your mind.' This is the first and greatest commandment. And the second is like it: 'Love your neighbor as yourself'" (Matthew 22:36–39).

The purpose of our being is greater than navigating the setbacks and unexpected turns of life. In all we do, we should seek to serve and love others. And that means being willing to give of ourselves and our experience to help someone else. This takes a servant's heart. "The greatest among you will be your servant," Jesus said in Matthew 23:11.

The wisdom you've earned—and are still earning—through the process of coming through your setback carries a hefty price tag. If you had the ability to go back in time and choose the events of your life, you probably would not have chosen for this setback to have happened. You've paid a high price to make a recovery, to set your life onto a new course, and to glorify God in the process. But I believe the ultimate gift back to God would be to allow the price you paid to also pay the price for someone else. How? By being open and transparent in sharing His love, His wisdom, and His mercy with those who cross your path.

Let Others See God Through You

Choosing transparency requires us to overcome three obstacles: pride, privacy, and pity.

Pride. Pride is about self-preservation. We'd rather not admit our struggles because we don't want people to see us in a less flattering light. Pride wants others to see our successes and never our failures, our strengths but not our weaknesses. However, when you truly accept God's grace and mercy, your heart has no room for pride. You're overflowing with delight in God's amazing grace.

Privacy. For sake of privacy, many people keep their struggles and triumphs to themselves. Privacy is sometimes simply an excuse to justify pride, while at other times privacy is about personality. Some people are naturally quiet and meek. Meekness is a godly quality, but false humility is not. I am not suggesting you boast about your recovery—far from it. However, don't be so private that God gets no glory.

Pity. The third potential obstacle to transparency is the fear that others will pity you. But if you are truly honest about all you're learning, if you're choosing to forge ahead in faith, and if you are trusting God to lead you into a better place in His time, then most people will not only cheer you on but will be inspired to face their own challenges with courage and resilience.

On a recent flight, I found myself in conversation with the gentleman sitting next to me. It was clear that he had experienced some tremendous material success in his life—including a successful business, professional sports career, and even a ten-thousand-square-foot mansion in the suburbs. But I found his mention of these external successes far less striking than his remarkable openness in discussing a series of financial setbacks that caused him to lose much of what he'd built.

In the process of losing the material symbols of his financial success, he was humbled. He'd been stripped of his previous arrogance. Before disaster struck, he said, he didn't have compassion for people who fell into financial challenges. "My philosophy," he explained, "was that if you just follow these rules and these steps, you'll be successful like me. But my setbacks taught me that sometimes there are things beyond your control that cause major setbacks. And God showed me that even if it is your fault, He forgives you and will restore you."

In the process of losing his money, this gentleman also lost his prideful attitude. As a result, God could use him on a greater level. Now he travels the country speaking to people about bouncing back financially.

This businessman didn't gain his transformed perspective overnight though, and most likely neither will you. Falling from a high point in life is a humbling experience, and the first reaction is often, *How can I hide this? How can I pretend everything is really okay?* The enemy would love for you to believe that a setback disqualifies you from many of the ways in which God wants to use you moving forward. But if you can be still and listen for God's voice, you'll hear Him nudging you toward the truth. If you can face the truth and accept it, pride will have no place in you. Being able to embrace that "it is what it is" empowers you to be free and authentic. You can be *you* and in being you, you can be a blessing to someone else who's facing a challenge.

In what way(s) is pride getting in the way of your helping others by sharing your story?

What would it look like for you to set aside that pride for the sake of God's glory?

Your Pain Is Not in Vain

Your transparency can actually free others to stop hiding from their own circumstances. Your example can give them the strength to face their fears and conquer their obstacles. "We are therefore Christ's ambassadors, as though God were making his appeal through us," 2 Corinthians 5:20 tells us.

As an ambassador, you demonstrate the power of God's love, mercy, healing, and grace. You have the opportunity to be a living, breathing example of the truth that nothing is impossible with God. What you have been through has the power to change lives, shift attitudes, give hope, and shed light. Most people never get to this level of recovery, but I believe you can.

Do you believe you can do all things through Christ who strengthens you? Then make sure your actions line up with that belief. God will bring opportunities into your path to be a blessing to others. Even at times when you are unaware other people are watching you, getting their cues for how to handle a crisis from how you handle yours—God is using you.

When you walk with God—when you seek to glorify Him—nothing you go through is in vain. As we near the end of our journey through these pages, we come to a profound question: *What is the purpose in your pain?*

How can the world be a little bit better because you have gone through what you've gone through? Jot down the first thoughts that come to you.

You remember Kevin, the resilient young man whose baseball hazing injury left him paralyzed? Kevin became a Christian during his last semester of college, nearly six years after the injury—and God has used him in ways he could never have imagined before his injury.

"I believe I have the gift of inspiration. I am an encourager," he explains. "People can just approach me and talk to me even though I use a wheelchair. I can talk to pretty much anyone, even though I am a quadriplegic. I think that gift has been a way for me to share my faith. I am able to witness about what Jesus has done for me. Even though what happened to me was tragic, I also have a lot to look forward to."

Kevin never gave up on his dreams of a professional career, marriage, and children. He didn't allow his fate as a quadriplegic to disqualify him from his dreams. Just as important, his attitude makes him an inspiring ambassador for Christ.

As I interviewed Kevin, he didn't have to try to inspire me. He *is* inspiration. It's who he is. His attitude. His victories. His family. His wife. So many aspects of his life speak volumes without his saying a word. And the lessons his life communicates inspire the countless people whose paths he crosses every day. He inspires them to be grateful, to not give up on their dreams, and to believe in the power of God to bring about miracles in their lives.

What about you? In what way(s) do you want your setback and recovery to inspire or help others?

Whether by your inspiring example, positive attitude with those in your inner circle, or passionate support for a cause that you champion, be intentional now about the ways in which your comeback will serve as your platform to share with others and express your gratitude for the incredible blessings you've received while navigating life's unexpected turns.

You Have Everything You Need

Use the Power of Your *Thoughts*

Focus your thoughts on how you will be better as a result of your setback. Identify the characteristic you believe God is nurturing in you through this experience, and make that the thought you return to when you need a boost of encouragement.

Use the Power of Your *Words*

Tell your story. Using the questions asked in this chapter, create your own narrative about how this experience has transformed you so far and how you want to see that transformation play out in the months and years to come.

Use the Power of Your *Actions*

Choose to be better, not bitter. Identify one action you can take today that expresses forgiveness, gratitude, or optimism in your situation.

Use the Power of *Relationships*

Talk it out. Choose someone you trust and have a conversation about the lessons you've learned and messages you believe God is offering through your challenges.

Use the Power of *Prayer*

God, thank You for your transformative power. Despite all that I have been through, I trust You to shape and mold me into the person You want me to be. Help me to be open to the opportunity for growth. Amen.

COACHING GUIDE

———◆———

As founder of the Coaching and Positive Psychology (CaPP) Institute, I've trained and developed personal and executive coaches from across the United States and around the world, equipping them to help people effectively move forward in their personal and professional lives. In the pages that follow, I draw on the principles I use daily with my clients to help you have powerful coaching conversations and keep moving forward in your own life.

I hope you have already used the self-coaching tools in each chapter of *Where Will You Go from Here?* to discover answers that will help you grow, take action, and find peace and joy in the midst of challenges. Now, I want to give you one more tool. As we've discussed, "reaching out" is a key part of resilience. Going it alone is highly overrated. While self-coaching is a useful skill you can continue to use throughout your life, you'll gain great benefits from engaging in a coaching conversation in the company of others.

This Coaching Guide is more than just a discussion guide. I encourage you to partner with at least one other person or—even better—use this guide with your book club, small group, or Bible study group. Consider initiating a group that brings together people who, like you, are experiencing an unexpected life shift, such as divorce, a change in employment, the death of a loved one, or perhaps a health crisis.

Whatever the nature of your group—whether it's just you and a friend who acts as your coach or whether you have several people participating together—the idea is to create informal coaching sessions that will spark fresh insights and creative thinking to help you move forward even when life doesn't go as planned.

To that end, I've provided targeted coaching questions based on each chapter of the book. In a confidential, supportive manner, whoever is in the role of the coach will ask these questions, providing sufficient time for participants to think and then talk through their answers. You'll want to do this over the span of several meetings or sessions; it would be too overwhelming to absorb and answer all of the questions in one sitting. In addition, spacing out the discussions will give participants the opportunity to process what they've learned and then take action based on their answers. Consider scheduling at least six sessions, covering no more than two chapters per session. Or you may want to plan on a full twelve sessions so the participants can spend plenty of time exploring the insights they gain from each chapter's questions.

If you are using the guide for a group of four or more, you may want to have one person lead the discussion, and then have the group break into pairs where one person initially serves as coach, then the participants switch roles. Set a time limit for each segment so everyone has a chance to both share and listen.

Here are a few additional guidelines to keep in mind:

1. The coach must listen more than he or she talks.

The coach's primary role is to serve as an active listener, who gives group members freedom to answer questions without chiming in with her own answers first. Coaching is about participants discovering the answers by listening to their own life and to the quiet voice of God's wisdom, not about someone else telling them what to do. So it is critical that the person acting as coach resist the urge to attempt to solve their challenges for them.

As an active listener, the coach should be empathetic, nonjudgmental, and intuitive. This may mean that, once the person being coached has had a chance to express himself or herself, the coach will sense the need for a follow-up question to help that person go even further in his thinking. Follow your intuition. Ask the obvious. Speak the truth in love.

2. Create a safe space.

Whether you use this guide with just one other person as your coach or in a group setting, each participant needs to agree up-front that everything will be kept confidential. Doing so will help you create a safe space for productive conversation.

Another important aspect of creating a safe space is to ban judgment from the conversation. In other words, the coach and others in the group agree not to react negatively to any situations that are shared. Remain neutral so the person being coached feels the freedom to be honest and open, without fear of being judged.

3. Focus forward.

You'll notice the questions in this Coaching Guide are focused on your present and your future, not the past. That is because coaching is not counseling or therapy. Coaching is about examining where you are *now* and identifying where you are heading. Keep the conversation focused forward. The session should center on next steps and goals, actions and decisions that will move you closer to your vision.

If you find yourself unable to do this, it may be an indication that professional counseling is needed. When you're dealing with the pain of an open wound, it's difficult to concentrate on future needs. Once your wound is healed, you may have a scar to show for it, but the scar won't demand your attention. You'll be free to focus forward.

We're ready to dive in to the coaching questions. You likely will find each session more productive if you review each chapter before you discuss the related questions.

Chapter 1—This Isn't the Way You Planned It: When Your World Turns Upside Down

Before you address the following questions, spend some time reviewing The Five Commitments on page 10.

1. Which of the Five Commitments resonates most powerfully with you, and why?

2. How will you use the commitment that resonates most strongly with you to triumph in the face of your challenges and opportunities?

3. What is the first step that you will take in that direction? When will you take that step?

Chapter 2—Where in the World Are You? How to Assess the Damage and Get Clear About Exactly Where You Are

1. Name up to three of the top challenges or opportunities you face right now. Be specific.

2. In what way(s) are you feeling disoriented? What unhealthy or unproductive thing(s) have you reached for in order to find some sense of stability or normalcy? What is a better alternative?

3. What would it look like for you to "get up" rather than "give up"? Make a list of the ways you can do this.

Chapter 3—How Did You End Up Here? Examining the Path That Led You Here Can Yield Crucial Clues About What to Do—and What Not to Do—Next

1. What lessons for your journey can you glean from Kevin Wolitzky's "Triumph Over Trials" story at the end of chapter 2?
2. What lesson(s) are being offered to you right now from your own situation? How will you apply the lesson(s) as you move forward?
3. What decision(s) are you tempted to make hastily? What will you do to consider your decision(s) more carefully?

Chapter 4—What Are You Most Afraid Of? Calling Out Your Fears Is the First Step to Conquering Them

1. What are your three biggest fears right now?
2. What else are you afraid of? In other words, what are you *not* saying because you're reluctant to give voice to it?
3. What people or things will help you unearth courage in the face of your biggest fear?
4. When was another time in your life that you exhibited courage in the face of fear?
5. Despite your fear(s), what will you muster the courage to do this week because you want to press forward?

Chapter 5—How Can You Regain Your Confidence? Finding Stability and Strength to Prepare for Your Comeback

1. What do you need to accept that you cannot change?
2. What specific aspects of your situation are within your power to change?

3. What three small goals will you set to initiate the changes you have the power to make?

4. What personal character strengths will you tap to accomplish these goals?

Chapter 6—Where Can You Turn for Help? Learning to Receive with Grace and Humility

1. What need(s) do you have right now that are not being met? Where could you find a positive, healthy source of help to meet those need(s)?

2. In what way(s) do you resist asking for help? What will you do to push past pride, fear, or other issues to ask anyway?

3. There are ways in which you have been helped without even asking. Think back to an act of kindness, a conversation, or situation that has blessed you in the midst of your setback. What help are you most grateful for?

Chapter 7—Where Will You Go from Here? Deciding Whether to Forge a New Path or Return to the Old One

1. If God were sitting here with you right now, what do you think He would tell you about where you need to go from here?

2. Do you need to forge a new path for your life or return to your previous path?

3. Based on your answer to the previous question, what does that new path and destination look like? In other words, what's your vision?

4. What milestones will you celebrate as you make progress on your path? How will you celebrate in a way that maximizes your positive emotion?

Chapter 8—Do You Need to Redefine Yourself? Gaining a Clearer Picture of Your Authentic Self and Coming to Terms with Your New Identity

1. In what way(s) do you need to redefine yourself? What's the old definition of you? In what specific aspects is that different from your new identity?

2. Revisit the four stages of an identity shift in chapter 8. In what way(s) are you clinging to the past? What is it time to let go of? What is it time to embrace?

3. Practice optimism and give yourself some credit for the good things in your life. In the midst of your setback, what personal decision or action are you most proud of? Why?

Chapter 9—What's the Best Way to Get There from Here? Designing Your Comeback, Step by Step

This discussion may take longer than the others, but it's absolutely crucial to moving forward. Be sure to allot enough time to answer each question thoroughly.

1. Think back to the vision and time line you crafted in chapter 9 and also to how you answered the identity questions in the chapter 8 discussion of this Coaching Guide. What specific goals have you sensed in your spirit that you need to set? Identify all of them.

2. What action steps will you need to take to support each goal?

3. What obstacles do you anticipate? Identify at least two or three. How will you overcome those obstacles if and when they come? (Remember, resilient people expect challenges will sometimes come and *believe* they have the ability to handle them.)

Chapter 10—Are Your Thoughts Holding You Back?
Thinking Carefully About How You Think

1. What is your most consistent pessimistic, counterproductive thought?

2. What productive, optimistic thought could you choose to think instead?

3. What tends to trigger that pessimistic thought? How do you react as a result of it (in other words, what do you say or do when that thought comes)? If the trigger came and you chose the productive, optimistic thought instead, how would you react differently?

4. Faith is the substance of things *hoped for.* What are you hoping for as you move forward? Paint a vivid picture of what you hope for, and write it down. Then together with your coach, pray a prayer asking God for the things you hope for.

Chapter 11—Why Don't You Feel Happier by Now?
Reclaiming Your Joy Even Before Your Comeback Is Complete

1. What brings you joy? How could you incorporate more of that into your life on a daily basis?

2. What is something you can do this week that you would look forward to? When will you do it?

3. Let's look at the seven ingredients in the "Recipe for Joy" in chapter 11. Which of these will you integrate into your action steps as you move forward? How will you keep yourself accountable?

Chapter 12—How Can You Find the Good in All This? Growing Through Your Trials, Not Just Going Through Them

1. What specific personal growth have you experienced as a result of your setback?
2. What good has come through this setback? (Please note: This is not to say that the setback itself was good, but that all things work together for good for those who love God and are called according to His purpose, and therefore, you can find something good even in the midst of the negative.)
3. How will you use your experience to help others? Be specific.

Author's Note

W hat a blessing it has been to walk with you through this turning point in your life. My hope is that you've gained some valuable emotional and psychological tools that will empower you to persevere as you journey toward your destiny.

I know the path you're on isn't the one you planned, but I also know that with God's guidance and grace, your character and strength will be deepened by this experience. By embracing this new life with courage and passion and resilience, you will have more appreciation and joy for whatever lies ahead. When setbacks strip us of all the "stuff" we thought we needed, we come to realize that true peace is not dependent on what we have or on what happens to us. It comes from placing our trust in God at all times, from choosing to keep on living and loving and believing, even in the face of our biggest fears.

Where will you go from here? My prayer is this:

May you find joy in the midst of your trials;

May you possess more than enough courage to conquer every fear that comes your way;

May you exercise the power to take every thought captive and line them up in divine order;

May your best days be yet to come—and may you recognize them and live them fully when they arrive.

I have been honored to walk with you on your journey during this pivotal season of your life. Let's not stop here. I would love to hear how this book has helped you, what you are doing differently in your life, and the strategies that best worked for you. Become a fan on Facebook and post your story or give your feedback. Follow me on Twitter. And I would love to continue inspiring you every single week with my free weekly e-newsletter, "The Coaching Session." "The Coaching Session" will give you timely, inspiring, practical ideas for thriving in life and work—and equip you with a week-by-week challenge and coaching question to keep you moving forward. Just go to www.valorieburton.com to subscribe. If you'd like to delve deeper through personal development training or coaching for yourself or employees in your company, visit the CaPP Institute Web site at www.cappinstitute.com.

Although this book is coming to an end for you, I hope you'll revisit these pages as often as you need to as you move forward!

Your coach and friend,

Valorie Burton

ACKNOWLEDGMENTS

K en Petersen, my publisher, who helped spark the idea for this book without even knowing that God had destined me to write it. Thank you.

Laura Barker, thank you for always believing in my work—and making it better. You are steady, patient, insightful, and delightful to work with!

Andrea Heinecke, my literary agent. Thank you for your efforts and guidance.

The team at the Positive Psychology Center and Applied Positive Psychology graduate program at the University of Pennsylvania, including Dr. James Pawelski and Debbie Swick, and especially Dr. Martin Seligman. Thank you for creating an inspiring opportunity for learning and growth for those of us who are practitioners. My experience at the University of Pennsylvania changed my life. I am so excited sharing this knowledge with my readers and audiences. To Dr. Karen Reivich, whose work in the field of resilience is transforming thousands of lives, thank you. *The Resilience Factor* and your training impacted my life at a time when I had to ask myself, *Where will you go from here?*

Thank you to my many friends and family who were there when I landed in the ditch, especially Mom (Leone Adger Murray) and Dad (Johnny Burton), Revs. Johnny and Billie Donald, John Lynell Baker, Kelly Young, Regina Butler, Quincey Heatley, and Elicia Brand-Leudemann.

Your prayers, wisdom, conversation, encouragement, and love lifted me. Thank you.

And I thank God for the opportunity to live out my calling and do work I love.

For you, the reader, I pray this work has blessed you when you most needed it.

Notes

Chapter 1

1. *Merriam-Webster Unabridged*, s.v. "temper," www.merriam-webster
   .com/dictionary/temper.

Chapter 2

1. Karen Reivich, PhD, and Andrew Shatté, PhD, *The Resilience Factor*
   (New York: Broadway, 2002), 3.
2. Kevin Wolitzky, personal telephone interview, July 14, 2010.

Chapter 3

1. Deanna Jones, personal telephone interview, November 23, 2010.

Chapter 4

1. Jacqueline Jakes, personal telephone interview, July 7, 2010.
2. In addition to having written *Tough Cookie*, Lillian Sparks is the
   author of *Don't Cry for Me*, a book for people who've lost loved ones;
   and *Parents Cry Too!*, a book Dr. James Dobson encouraged her to
   write to help parents of disabled children.
3. Lillian Sparks, personal telephone interview, November 30, 2010.

Chapter 5

1. Attributed to Reinhold Niebuhr. But there is some question as to
   whether he was the original author.

2. Suzanne C. Kobasa and Mark C. Puccetti (1983), "Personality and social resources in stress resistance," *Journal of Personality and Social Psychology* 45:4 (October 1983): 839–50, quoted in Karen Reivich, PhD, and Andrew Shatté, PhD, *The Resilience Factor* (New York: Broadway, 2002), 191.

3. Jacqueline Jakes, *God's Trophy Women* (New York: Warner Faith, 2006).

4. Jacqueline Jakes, personal telephone interview, July 7, 2010.

5. Christopher Peterson and Martin E. P. Seligman, *Character Strengths and Virtues* (New York: Oxford University Press, 2004), 28–30.

6. Faith Proietti, personal telephone interview, November 24, 2010.

Chapter 6

1. Tom Rath, *Vital Friends: The People You Can't Afford to Live Without* (New York: Gallup Press, 2006).

2. Mayo Clinic staff. "Depression (major depression): Symptoms," www.mayoclinic.com/health/depression/DS00175/DSECTION=symptoms.

3. "Richard" [name withheld by mutual agreement], personal interview.

Chapter 7

1. Barbara L Fredrickson, "The Role of Positive Emotions in Positive Psychology: The Broaden and Build Theory of Positive Emotions," *American Psychologist* 56:3 (March 2001): 218–226, www.unc.edu/peplab/publications/role.pdf.

2. Valorie Burton, *What's Really Holding You Back?* (Colorado Springs, CO: WaterBrook, 2005), 64–66.

3. Roland S. Martin, personal telephone interview, June 30, 2010.

Chapter 8

1. Sonja Lyubomirsky, *The How of Happiness* (New York: Penguin, 2007), 20.

2. Taft Quincey Heatley, personal telephone interview, December 9, 2010.

Chapter 10

1. Karen Reivich, PhD, and Andrew Shatté, PhD, *The Resilience Factor* (New York: Broadway, 2002), 65–94.

2. Martin Seligman, PhD, *Learned Optimism* (New York: Vintage, 2006), 14–16.

3. Seligman, PhD, *Learned Optimism*, 44.

4. Ronetta Slaughter, personal telephone interview, July 14, 2010.

Chapter 11

1. Barbara L. Fredrickson, PhD, *Positivity* (New York: Crown Archetype, 2009).

2. Fredrickson, *Positivity*, 59–62.

3. Fredrickson, *Positivity*, 21.

4. Fredrickson, *Positivity*, 32, 130.

5. Sonja Lyubomirsky, *The How of Happiness* (New York: Penguin, 2007), 20–22.

6. Robert A. Emmons and Michael E. McCullough, "Counting Blessings Versus Burdens: An Experimental Investigation of Gratitude and Subjective Well-Being in Daily Life," *Journal of Personality and Social Psychology* 84:2 (2003): 377–389. Robert A. Emmons, *Thanks! How the New Science of Gratitude Can Make You Happier* (New York: Houghton Mifflin, 2007), 11.

7. James A. Blumenthal, PhD, et al, "Effects of Exercise Training on Older Patients with Major Depression," *The Archives of Internal Medicine* 159 (October 25, 1999): 2349–2356.

8. Tom Rath and Jim Harter, *Well Being: The Five Essential Elements* (New York: Gallup, 2010).

9. Ruth Puleo, personal telephone interview, November 26, 2010.

Chapter 12

1. Lawrence Calhoun and Richard Tedeschi, "Posttraumatic Growth: Future Directions" in R. Tedeschi and L. Calhoun, eds., *Posttraumatic Growth: Positive Changes in the Aftermath of Crisis* (Mahwah, NJ: Lawrence Earlbaum, 1998), 215–240. Lawrence Calhoun and Richard Tedeschi, "Posttraumatic Growth: Conceptual Issues," in R. Tedeschi and L. Calhoun, eds., *Posttraumatic Growth: Positive Changes in the Aftermath of Crisis* (Mahwah, NJ: Lawrence Earlbaum, 1998), 1–22.

2. Lawrence Calhoun and Richard Tedeschi, *Facilitating Posttraumatic Growth* (Mahwah, NJ: Lawrence Erlbaum, 1999), 10.

3. William Shakespeare, *As You Like It,* Act 2, Scene 1.

4. Jacqueline Jakes, *Jacqueline's Spiritual Jewels* (Shippensburg, PA: Destiny Image, 2006), 17.

5. Laura A. King, "The Health Benefits of Writing About Life Goals," *Personality and Social Psychology Bulletin,* 27:7 (July 2001): 798–807.